Find Your Promised Land

Find Your Promised Land

Getting Through Your Wilderness

ISRAEL KIM

 Unless otherwise identified, Scripture quotations are from the New King James Version. Please note that Destiny Image's publishing style capitalizes certain pronouns in Scripture that refer to the Father, Son, and Holy Spirit, and may differ from some publishers' styles. Emphasis within Scripture quotations is the author's own. Take note that the name satan and related names are not capitalized. We choose not to acknowledge him, even to the point of violating grammatical rules.

DESTINY IMAGE® PUBLISHERS, INC.

P.O. Box 310, Shippensburg, PA 17257-0310

"Speaking to the Purposes of God for This Generation and for the Generations to Come."

This book and all other Destiny Image, Revival Press, Mercy Place, Fresh Bread, Destiny Image Fiction, and Treasure House books are available at Christian bookstores and distributors worldwide.

For a U.S. bookstore nearest you, call **1-800-722-6774.**

For more information on foreign distributors, call **717-532-3040.**

Or reach us on the Internet: **www.destinyimage.com**

ISBN 10: 0-7684-2836-X

ISBN 13: 978-0-7684-2836-0

For Worldwide Distribution, Printed in the U.S.A.

1 2 3 4 5 6 7 8 9 10 11 / 13 12 11 10 09

Acknowledgments

I would like to thank my wife and daughter. I appreciate all the sacrifices you both made. I wouldn't be the man of God today if it wasn't for your love and sacrifice. With your help, I was able to finish what God called me to do.

I would also like to thank my spiritual sons, Jacob Kim and Robert MacMullen, for your help in putting this book together. You have been faithful and committed to the Kingdom of God. May you increase in God's anointing and blessings.

I would also like to thank my colleagues and friends. You've been very inspiring in my life. I really thank the Lord that we were able to build godly relationships over the years. May the Lord bless your lives and ministries.

Endorsements

One of the most important truths for Christians to understand is God's ways of perfecting His people. Everyone who is called to be joint-heirs with Christ Jesus and reign with Him must go through the wilderness of testing. Our great forefather, Abraham, went through seven major tests before God changed his prophesied destiny from a prophetic promise to a sovereign oath by God Himself. This book could make the difference in whether you become a full overcomer. Receive this truth, for it will make you free to fulfill your destiny.

—Dr. Bill Hamon
Bishop of Christian International Ministries Network
Author of *Who Am I and Why Am I Here?*
Santa Rosa Beach, Florida

I found Israel Kim's writing to be clear, spiritual, and full of depth. I was very encouraged by what I read and think that he has a great calling to not only influence by preaching, teaching, and discipling, but in writing. May God use this book in a special way. I hope Kim does not forget the redemption of Israel as his influence in the Church grows.

—Dr. Daniel Juster
Founder/President of Tikkun Ministries International
Jerusalem, Israel

In his book *Find Your Promised Land,* apostle Israel Kim has opened up some wonderful revelations concerning the wilderness walk. These truths have long been ignored by much of the Body of Christ. Any reader will find this to be a challenging 21st century book for 21st century Christians. I've been in the ministry for 48 years, yet Israel Kim's book has brought a new understanding to me. I endorse and highly recommend *Find Your Promised Land.*

—Dr. Robert H. Lemon
Harvest Fire International
Canton, Michigan
www.hfi-newday.net

The wilderness experience is viewed by many as a time of dryness, confusion, and frustration. However, God uses wilderness events in our lives to cause us to become the person He has called us to be. By comparing our personal wilderness experience to that of the Israelites, Israel Kim, in his book *Find Your Promised Land,* reveals a much greater plan for our lives.

The wilderness is not a place of barrenness and death, but a place where God releases His supernatural power to produce believers who live life at its fullest and best! *Find Your Promised Land* should be read by all who desire to break out of isolation, emptiness, and defeat into a life that is transformed by the supernatural power of God!

—Barbara Wentroble
Founder/President of International Breakthrough Ministries
Author of *Prophetic Intercession: Praying With Authority*
Ft. Worth, Texas

All of us experience the wilderness season at some time in our lives. This book by Israel Kim is filled with practical wisdom that will help you embrace the wilderness experience, which will prepare you for the next season in your life. Expect the Lord to speak to you as you read this book. It is anointed and written with humility and transparency.

—Larry Kreider
Author and International Director of DOVE International

Doing God's will is the best sign of God's servants, so experiencing suffering for the cause of Christ is still the highest form of faith and the most glorious Christian achievement. For this reason, Israel Kim's *Find Your Promised Land* is highly recommended. It is thoroughly biblical, theologically sound, and very practical. Heroes of the Bible had this wilderness experience. God is looking for this kind of servant. I recommend this book highly.

—Paul Ariga
President of All Japan Revival Mission,
Revival Biblical Seminary

When most of us hear the word wilderness, we turn and run or rebuke the thought. Israel Kim masterfully weaves

God's divine purposes of the wilderness throughout this book. You will find yourself desiring to become more like Christ and choosing to let God change you and renew your mind. Learn how to systematically dismantle satan's assaults and strategies that are designed to thwart your destiny. As you read, God will stir up a passion in you to no longer shun the wilderness experience, but to embrace it. You are destined for greatness.

—Tommi Femrite, Author and Founding Apostle
GateKeepers International &
Apostolic Intercessors Network
Colorado Springs, Colorado

Israel Kim's new book is a must read for those wanting to know a very important way of God. God takes us out of Egypt so He can take us into Canaan, the land of God's purpose and destiny. But we had better know about the wilderness, that time when we are on the way to maturity but not quite there yet. How we handle the wilderness experiences determines how quickly God can get us to our land of promises. Read on and get to your land of milk and honey...quickly!

—Dr. Ed Delph
Nationstrategy
Phoenix, Arizona

Contents

Foreword

A book on the wilderness experience in order to find a promised land is a book for all of us. Why? We have all gone through our wilderness experiences in our quest to serve God and reach our destiny, and there may be other such experiences yet to come. We may not like them, but we cannot avoid them. When we do go into the wilderness, one question should be paramount in our mind: Why am I here? What is God's purpose? That is why I am so grateful that Israel Kim has written a whole book on *Find Your Promised Land.*

It is very important to realize that, even when we are living a life pleasing to God, we will have our times in the wilderness. And it is God who may move us there. For example, Jesus did not plan to take Himself into the wilderness for 40 days, but it was the Holy Spirit who took Him there. The purpose was so that Jesus could prove to the Father that He was obedient. In order to do so, He resisted the three temptations offered to Him by the devil himself. Through that ordeal, not only did Jesus learn obedience, but he also identified more closely with us. When Jesus sees us go through troublesome times, He knows what we are going through.

When God sent Israel through the Red Sea into the wilderness, it was a different story. That wilderness journey was not supposed to last 40 years, as it turned out doing. The road through the wilderness was supposed to take Israel straight to the Promised Land. However, the leaders disobeyed God. The priest, Aaron, turned to idolatry. Moses struck the rock when God had told him to speak to the rock. The result? An entire generation had to suffer in the wilderness for the rest of their lives, and only the next generation could move into the Promised Land.

What we can learn from this is what Israel Kim explains so well in his book. As you will see from Dr. Kim's testimony, there are good ways to face up to a wilderness experience, and there are wrong ways. Trusting God and not disobeying Him are the keys to reaping great positive benefits from whatever might come your way. True, it is not always easy, but the wisdom you glean from this book will give you new hope and promise.

My suggestion is that you keep a number of copies of *Find Your Promised Land* on hand. When friends and family members are entering difficult times, give them a copy of this book along with your own words of encouragement. Help them take their eyes off the wilderness and look toward the future. They will love you for it!

—C. Peter Wagner, Chancellor
Wagner Leadership Institute

Introduction

AS we reflect upon our callings, many of us will note that we have experienced tumultuous seasons where the events, people, and circumstances surrounding these moments made little sense. It is during these times that many of us have called upon the Lord, and asked, *why is this happening?* Or perhaps, *what have I done to deserve this?* With no tangible answer we have slipped into despair, losing momentum or even sitting down, imagining an unassailable fortress before us. To counteract our lack of progress, we embark upon an adventure of self-pity or anger, formulating a bevy of excuses to convince ourselves and the world that our situation is extraordinary and no one else can understand.

Even though you face these difficult challenges, there is great news! God has not given up on you; He never has and never will. The biblical truth is this: He is with you in every situation of your life. The Word tells us that Jesus will never leave you.

For He Himself has said, "I will never leave you nor forsake you" (Hebrews 13:5).

God has not given up on you;
He never has and never will.

Beloved, do not think it strange concerning the fiery trial which is to try you, as though some strange thing happened to you; but rejoice to the extent that you partake of Christ's sufferings, that when His glory is revealed, you may also be glad with exceeding joy (1 Peter 4:12-13).

As you grow, you must begin to learn these "desert" experiences are for your ultimate benefit. They are interludes where God is shaping you. Therefore, if you only look at your current circumstances, you will miss out on what God wants to make you. He sees your potential and understands the path necessary to fulfill His work. Indeed, God could easily eradicate the situation, but through it, He sees a work that has been forged according to His plans.

As we will note throughout this book, the Bible provides numerous examples of how God uses the inadequate, sinful, and unintelligent because He forgives our sinful nature and examines our heart. For when God examines us, He is reviewing our potential. It is specifically for this reason that the Scriptures counsel us not to consider it strange when trials come. Every time we feel that there is no hope, we need to remember God is in the process of making us into the people He called us to be. That is why miracles cannot happen unless there are issues, and when we face adversity, we need to expect miracles and believe that all things are for our good and well-being. As our Creator, He knows exactly what it will take to transform us from glory to glory.

> *But we all, with unveiled face, beholding as in a mirror the glory of the Lord, are being transformed into the same image from glory to glory, just as by the Spirit of the Lord* (2 Corinthians 3:18).

Why does God want to change, mold, and shape us? It is because, since we are in Christ, He wants to restore what was taken the moment Adam fell. It is the restoration of all the power and authority found in the Garden of Eden with an understanding of it so we can resist temptation (unlike Adam and Eve) and fulfill His purpose.

Indeed, we must know that a provision of this magnitude requires responsibility too. As humankind grows more corrupt and wicked, God wants us to deliver people out of this corruption and wickedness. Before we can be used to deliver people, we first must be separated, consecrated, and purified by God. We need to be refined and understand that the journey before us will take us to our final destination, fully prepared to execute the perfect will of God in our lives.

> *And we know that all things work together for good to those who love God, to those who are the called according to His purpose* (Romans 8:28).

Chapter 1

The Story of Egypt

The Story of Israel in Egypt

MOST of us are familiar with the Israelite story of Egyptian captivity and subsequent desert experience before reaching the Promised Land. The fruit of that 40-year journey and promise actually began as a seed that was established in the relationship between Joseph and Pharaoh. When Joseph died and a new pharaoh was installed, God began writing a new chapter in Israel's history that ultimately defined it as His chosen nation.

> *Now there arose a new king over Egypt, who did not know Joseph. And he said to his people, "Look, the people of the children of Israel are more and mightier than we; come, let us deal shrewdly with them, lest they multiply and it happen, in the event of war, that they also join our enemies and fight against us and so go up out of the land." Therefore they set taskmasters over them*

to afflict them with their burdens. And they built for Pharaoh supply cities, Pithom ad Raamses. But the more they afflicted them, the more they multiplied and grew. And they were in dread of the children of Israel (Exodus 1:8-12).

As Egyptian fears of the Israelites increased, harsher policies and punishments were instituted to sequester their emerging power. However, from this place the future Jewish nation began seeking a Deliverer who would ease their burden. You of course know that God heard His people and began developing a man whose character and talents could accomplish this task. That man, Moses, was himself a neophyte for he only had a limited understanding of his Hebrew identity.

Now it came to pass in those days, when Moses was grown, that he went out to his brethren and looked at their burdens. And he saw an Egyptian beating a Hebrew, one of his brethren. So he looked this way and that way and when he saw no one, he killed the Egyptian and hid him in the sand. And when he went out the second day, behold, two Hebrew men were fighting and he said to the one who did the wrong; "Why are you striking your companion?" Then he said; "Who made you a prince and a judge over us? Do you intend to kill me as you killed the Egyptian?" So Moses feared and said, "Surely this thing is known!" When Pharaoh heard of this matter, he sought to kill Moses. But Moses fled from the face of Pharaoh and dwelt in the land of Midian (Exodus 2:11-15).

The Story of Moses

It was not until Moses faced persecution and a death sentence that God chose to mold him for the fulfillment of his ultimate purpose. Even though he had extensive academic and political skill, he was not ready to lead the Hebrew nation. Therefore, it would not be for another 40 years until the angel of the Lord called him back to deliver His chosen people.

> *And Moses was learned in all the wisdom of the Egyptians, and was mighty in words and deeds. Now when he was forty years old, it came into his heart to visit his brethren, the children of Israel. And seeing one of them suffer wrong, he defended and avenged him who was oppressed and struck down the Egyptian. For he supposed that his brethren would have understood that God would deliver them by his hand but they did not understand. And the next day he appeared to two of them as they were fighting and tried to reconcile them, saying, "Men, you are brethren; why do you wrong one another?" But he who did his neighbor wrong pushed him away saying, "Who made you a ruler and a judge over us? Do you want to kill me as you did the Egyptian yesterday?" Then at this saying, Moses fled and became a dweller in the land of Midian, where he had two sons. And when forty years had passed, an Angel of the Lord appeared to him in a flame of fire in a bush, in the wilderness of Mount Sinai* (Acts 7:22-30).

From a post-modern perspective, it is easy to speculate why it took Moses so long to return. It is easy to assume that family duties or other plans delayed his return. But in retrospect, I believe God was training him for a mission of tremendous importance, a mission that very few could ever appreciate or envision.

It was during this "Midian experience" that God chose to strip Moses of his Egyptian mentality, supplanting a lifetime of cult culture and religious practice with His wisdom and holiness. Critical to this task was the establishment of a relationship between man and God amid the plethora of spiritual deities inhabiting Egypt and Palestine.

Critical to this task was the establishment of a relationship between man and God.

In addition to this spiritual transformation, this desert respite was designed to produce a bold minister/advocate/leader of unquestionable credibility. As the Jewish "father of ministry," Moses' authority, actions, and manner would need to be irrefutable. In spite of his personal fears ("I am not capable or qualified" statements), God's relationship with Moses was unfailing; and in the deepest of times, God reassured Moses that He was going to be with him (providing support from Aaron).

Then Moses said to the Lord; "O my Lord, I am not eloquent, neither before nor since You have spoken to Your servant; but I am slow of speech and slow of tongue." So the Lord said to him; "Who has made man's mouth? Or who makes the mute, the deaf, the seeing, or the blind? Have not I, the Lord? Now therefore, go

> *and I will be with your mouth and teach you what you shall say." But he said; "O my Lord, please send by the hand of whomever else You may send." So the anger of the Lord was kindled against Moses and He said; "Is not Aaron the Levite your brother? I know that he can speak well. And look, he is also coming out to meet you. When he sees you, he will be glad in his heart. Now you shall speak to him and put the words in his mouth. And I will be with your mouth and with his mouth and I will teach you what you shall do. So he shall be your spokesman to the people. And he himself shall be as a mouth for you, and you shall be to him as God"* (Exodus 4:10-16).

After a series of meetings and subsequent supernatural catastrophes, Pharaoh released the Hebrew nation for what should have been a short two-week journey from Egypt to modern Israel. However it is safe to assume that Pharaoh soon reassessed the political cost and recognized the strategic implications of his decision.

For Pharaoh the Hebrew exodus was a political disaster that would destabilize the region, undermine his authority and invite an assault from his adversaries. To swiftly remedy this, Pharaoh gave chase, with his chariot army ultimately trapping the tribes against the Red Sea. But as the tactical battle unfolded and the Egyptian army raced into the watery breach, God's earlier promises to Moses were fulfilled, resulting in the Egyptian army's total destruction. This annihilation had a two-fold effect. First, the tribes no longer faced a vengeful and highly mobile threat from a leader whose ultimate goal was their complete obliteration. Second, and more importantly the back door and return to any "imagined and romanticized" Egyptian sanctuary was closed. From this point forward, the people could only move forward to meet the Lord at Mount Sinai.

Points to Ponder

1. Do you ever feel as if you are on a journey that only God can define for you? Are you ready to follow Him wherever He leads?

2. Are you allowing God to develop your talents and skills so you can fulfill your God-given destiny?

3. What personal fears are holding you back from fulfilling your potential?

Chapter 2

From Egypt to the Wilderness

Living in the Flesh

As you study Hebrew life in Egypt, the situation attests to the sophistication of satan's plan to steal from God's children. During this period, Egyptian demands increased and freedom diminished to the point where nothing was safe, for even the lives of newborn children were in jeopardy. Yet through all of this, God knew the suffering of His people.

However, for today the Egypt of the past refers to our "present day flesh," which can be defined as the place of falling short of God's glory. In Egypt there was no presence of the true God, and people lived in the flesh without His protection. Therefore the enemy was constantly attacking and consuming generations of victims. This example tells us that if we continue to live in the flesh, we will be devoured by satan and his legions as well.

If we continue to live in the flesh, we will be devoured by satan and his legions as well.

And the Lord God formed man of the dust of the ground, and breathed into his nostrils the breath of life; and man became a living being (Genesis 2:7).

That which is born of the flesh is flesh, and that which is born of the Spirit is spirit (John 3:6).

The warning is this: each time you venture from God's protection, the enemy has a right to attack you. He will show no hesitation, grace, or mercy and is consistently looking for an open door. It is for this reason you need to maintain vigilance, for you do not know the time or place, yet you know he uses all means to lure you. Therefore, you must constantly remind yourself that living in the flesh is a place without divine power or protection, for Jehovah does not live in the flesh but in the Spirit.

Living in the flesh, perhaps thinking you can go your own way, will always make you disobedient and is in fact a point of rebellion. Fleshly and consistently hard-hearted attitudes only serve to invite attack. As the Bible states:

But each one is tempted when he is drawn away by his own desires and enticed. Then, when desire has conceived, it gives birth to sin; and sin when it is full-grown, brings forth death (James 1:14-15).

Jehovah does not live in the flesh, but in the Spirit.

Therefore do not let sin reign in your mortal body, that you should obey it in its lusts. For sin shall not have dominion over you, for you are not under law but under grace (Romans 6:12,14).

And you He made alive, who were dead in trespasses and sins, in which you once walked according to the course of this world, according to the prince of the power of the air, the spirit who now works in the sons of disobedience, among whom also we all once conducted ourselves in the lusts of our flesh, fulfilling the desires of the flesh and of the mind and were by nature children of wrath, just as the others (Ephesians 2:1-3).

Within these last three Scriptures, the Lord is warning you not to give sin any opportunity to establish a foothold, for if you do, you have literally chosen to return to Egypt. Real freedom is the understanding that you must move under the hedge of protection that only God can offer.

If you do well, will you not be accepted? And if you do not do well, sin lies at the door. And its desire is for you, but you should rule over it (Genesis 4:7).

Living in Strongholds

If you study the Hebrew meaning of *Egypt,* it is characterized as a place of *adversity, power, bondage, or stronghold.* When you apply this definition to modern life, it becomes apparent that before you accepted Christ, you were exposed to some level of Egyptian rhetoric. That is to say, an idiom of worldly knowledge that is counterproductive to the true Word of the living God.

Real freedom is the understanding that you must move under the hedge of protection that only God can offer.

Much like when the Egyptians ruled the Israelites, you were in bondage, but unlike those times, most of you never consciously believed you were the enemy's servant. Yet by default, he was your master and you were his slave. As with the Israelites, his ability to create condemnation caused you to cringe in fear and led you to believe that you would face major consequences if you disobeyed or cried out for true freedom.

This fear has caused you to do his bidding and commit sins against God, others, and yourself. The same way satan rebelled against God and introduced sin to a willing community of participants, he has convinced many to believe that all things are possible without God. This speaks to a planted seed of pride that argues, *you know better and you deserve your independence,* rather than submitting to a viable and healthy relationship with your Lord and Savior.

Salvation Belongs to God

So then, what was God's true purpose for liberating the Israelites? Simply stated, it was for the salvation of His people and future generations. God wanted to save His people from the power of the enemy, and today He wants to free us from our old Egyptian bondage through His unparalleled grace.

> *For by grace you have been saved through faith, and that not of yourselves; it is the gift of God* (Ephesians 2:8).

For once you are saved, you are different, and a welcome participant in the Kingdom of God. You are God's Kingdom people and with this knowledge come blessings.

> *Blessed be the God and Father of our Lord Jesus Christ, who has blessed us with every spiritual blessing in the heavenly places in Christ* (Ephesians 1:3).

> ***But you are a chosen generation, a royal priesthood, a holy nation, His own special people,*** *that you may proclaim the praises of Him who called you out of darkness into His marvelous light, who once were not a people but are now the people of God, who had not obtained mercy but now have obtained mercy* (1 Peter 2:9-10).

God's Word comments that you are a chosen generation and that He made you priests with a royal heritage. Through this, He made you a holy nation in this world, to be His own special people. God saw in you something worth saving, so much so, that He sent His only Son to redeem you.

The Crossing of the Red Sea

What then is the significance of crossing the Red Sea and why didn't God just have them walk around it, or go through some other experience? In short it is because this catastrophic event served the dual purpose of freeing the Hebrew nation and forcing them to rely upon God.

The Red Sea experience represents the changes in your life as you cross over from the "secular world" and seek to find the Kingdom of God.

When God opened the Red Sea to permit a dry land crossing and ultimately trap and kill His earthly enemies, a deeper meaning sprang forth from its depths. Today, the Red Sea experience represents the changes in your life as you cross over from the "secular world" and seek to find the Kingdom of God. On the near shore you were a disobedient child. Accepting Christ Jesus' sacrifice provides a bridge or path that enables you to cross over from a life of inevitable torment to live as a child of light and obedience.

On this path you experience freedom from condemnation because His crucifixion and death rose above the roar of the enemy that you perceived to be around you. When Jesus said, "It is finished," He announced that all your enemies were defeated. That is why if you miss the experience of the Cross, you will never understand His truth and you will be blinded to a new life of freedom in Him.

You experience freedom from condemnation because His crucifixion and death rose above the roar of the enemy.

> *Therefore, brethren,* ***having boldness to enter the Holiest by the blood of Jesus, by a new and living way*** *which He consecrated for us, through the veil, that is, his flesh, and having a High Priest over the house of God, let us draw near with a true heart in full assurance of faith, having our hearts sprinkled from an evil conscience and our bodies washed with pure water. Let us hold fast the confession of our hope without wavering, for He who promised is faithful* (Hebrews 10:19-23).

It is the Cross experience that allows you to come boldly to the throne of God and say publicly that you need His help. In this modern era it is difficult to think of coming to a throne or actually visiting a king. Spiritually, you do it by dying on the Cross each day and resurrecting with Him as well. Through this new living arrangement, the enemy will not be able to touch you, for when you worship or sit at God's feet, you reside in the "cleft of the rock." This special and unique place is at the heart of a relationship with Him. It is a place of true love and consistent communion with your Abba Father.

Incident With the Witch Coven

The power of such a relationship should never be underestimated. I have personally experienced that hedge of protection and being hidden in the cleft of His rock. In 1988, a Quincy, Illinois, Christian television station invited me to share the vision God had given to me regarding the future of the United States. Even though my interview was only planned for 30 minutes, this powerful segment was extended for an additional 30 minutes and was broadcast by 128 stations. During this period, I vividly described how God had shown me and others how He was planning to fill seven U.S. sports stadiums with worshipers.

At the completion of this period of intense prayer and fasting, I was completely delivered from the oppression.

After this powerful national declaration, I returned home and within a week I lost some physical strength. I was neither sick nor fatigued, and the loss of strength became alarming. So I prayed in the Spirit and the Lord showed me that I had been standing in the middle of a witch coven. He further showed me that in the supernatural, they had surrounded me, lifted their hands, and spoke curses against me.

The Lord showed me that when I shared the vision about America and the world, the witch coven began casting spells and bringing curses upon my life. The Lord told me that to break this curse, I was to fast for seven days. At the completion of this period of intense prayer and fasting, I was completely delivered from the oppression. Even though the witches were casting powerful spells, it was only temporary. Just as with the Israelites in Egypt, God heard my cry for deliverance and most important when He answered, I obeyed.

Jesus' death means that God has already taken care of something that man has been struggling with for many years. The crucifixion experience is your ticket to a life without fear because His death was the sacrifice that ended the effectiveness of the enemy's weapons.

The Wilderness

I can only imagine the incredible panorama on the far shores of the Red Sea after God closed the breech and destroyed the chariot army. The horrific scene must have been an incredible demonstration of God's power as the waves crashed upon Pharaoh's men, equipment, and horses.

Yet even as the tribes celebrated their newfound freedom, a realization must have come to mind: they were now trapped in the desert, far away from fertile soil. With the Red Sea closed there was no way back, and in a strange paradox their newfound liberty could also lead to their death.

As they moved beyond the eastern shore toward the desert, the Scripture tells us that God manifested His presence.

> *And the Lord went before them by day in* ***a pillar of cloud to lead the way and by night in a pillar of fire to give them light, so as to go by day and night.*** *He did not take away the pillar of cloud by day or the pillar of fire by night from before the people* (Exodus 13:21-22).

From a modern perspective when you read the Scriptures, you can easily review the situation and openly question, how did the Israelites mess this up? Perhaps the real answer is this: even with all of the vast power demonstrated before them, they never realized or fully comprehended that it was God who was leading them. Instead, their focus was on the adventure of crossing the desert versus the wilderness before them.

Now it was time for His Word to strip them of their slave mentality and give them a fresh identity.

Now comes the next phase, the wilderness. The Hebrew word *mipara* is defined as *God's command, God's declaration, or Word of God. Desert* means *empty heaven.* God wanted to fill something in their lives. As stated previously, just as Moses had been educated in the highest Egyptian courts, God's people had also been educated under a similar system. Now it was time for His Word to strip them of their slave mentality and give them a fresh identity. The way God planned to do this was to purge them of their fleshly lifestyle. That is why the wilderness represents your "soul." It is your soul that needs to change. Once it changes, you can then begin to prosper.

> *Beloved, I pray that you may prosper in all things and be in health, just as your soul prospers* (3 John 1:2).

Your soul contains three components: knowledge, emotion, and will. In order for you to progress, these three must change. Your knowledge of the secular world is everything that you have learned academically or from society that does not follow God's truth. This is the knowledge you have before you believed in Jesus. After you believe in Jesus, you have to change your knowledge of the world to that of God's knowledge. Your emotion is where you choose to follow your feelings or instincts. Your will is the urge to control your own life and to make your own decisions. All these represent your human nature, but God wants your soul to be changed. Jesus came not to do His will but the will of the Father.

> *Incline your ear, and come to Me. Hear, and your soul shall live; And I will make an everlasting covenant with you—the sure mercies of David* (Isaiah 55:3).

It was during this wilderness experience that God began to provide His chosen nation with a period of cleansing. Their human nature and flesh were being stripped away so that the emptiness could be replaced with God's presence. God was putting His commandments in them and filling their empty heart with the Word of God. When God was filling them with His Words, He was showing them who they were and why God brought them out. This emptiness that He wanted to fill was the Garden of Eden. In the Garden there was constant joy and gladness. What God wanted to restore was people's true identity because we sometimes find our identity from what we do rather than from where we come from.

In the Garden, there was constant joy and gladness.

Just as He did for the Israelites, God wants to eliminate your worldly knowledge, for in reality, it is irrelevant. What is important in the wilderness is the transformation process into God's truth. Although frustrating, it is this period that teaches you the essence of finding fulfillment only in God.

Points to Ponder

1. Do you believe that when Jesus said, "It is finished," He announced that all your enemies were defeated?

2. "With the Red Sea closed, there was no way back, and in a strange paradox, their newfound liberty could also lead to their death." Have there been times when you faced a situation like this? Did you call on God to see you through?

3. Do you think people in the Western world are identified by what they do or where they come from? Why?

Chapter 3

What Is the Wilderness?

BEFORE the Israelites could enter the Promised Land and receive their inheritance as God's chosen nation, they first needed to cross the Sinai Desert. Most historians and academics agree that this journey from the western shores of the Red Sea to Palestine should have taken no more than two weeks. Yet instead of 14 days, the Hebrew nation spent the next 40 years wandering around this faceless terrain. So the logical questions are: "What took 39 years to accomplish?" and "What happened to the first generation of liberated Hebrews?" Surely, they were not simply wandering or lost in the desert.

The study of the Pentateuch clearly demonstrates that during these stages of slavery, liberation, and transition, God was seeking a nation of worshipers who were completely dependent upon Him. Even as modern 21st century readers, you can see a pattern where God was consistently looking to bring the Hebrews into a closer and deeper relationship. However, for Him the concept of time and patience are completely different and as a loving parent who spends countless hours correcting and training, you observe a heavenly Father with the same enduring patience and persistence. It's not hard to imagine that for the Israelites, this period of training and correction took 40 years and spanned two generations. After all, He was working with flesh and the Hebrews were not far removed from their Egyptian experience which produced hardened hearts, pride, and stiff necks. Scripture illuminates how they consistently desired the things of the past (Egypt), completely forgetting God's mighty works of liberation and freedom.

Does it seem like God is taking decades to lead you toward your destiny?

But the questions for you today are: Are you experiencing anything similar to the first generation of free Hebrews? Does it seem like God is taking decades to lead you toward your destiny? Are you on the verge of hardening your heart due to what you perceive as lack of progress or fulfillment?

You may wonder if God is being slow with His promises in your life but in reality God is waiting for you to act with a proper attitude. Don't ever forget that God wants to change your character, and He has shown with the Hebrew nation that time lines are His alone.

Characteristics of the Wilderness Journey

Many people who attend Bible-based churches hear sermons exhorting them to recognize that God is leading them on a journey. Yet I suspect that for many people these words mean very little. In our flesh we prefer to avoid situations that conjure up a "wilderness" and choose to imagine ourselves communing with God in some paradise-like setting. Yet since Adam's fall, our journey toward holiness cannot avoid the difficult times. As a believer we can trust God to bring us to the place, just like the Israelites, where He wants us to be. We should not make every bad circumstance something negative. He wants to change us through these events and do something in our lives that brings glory to Him and ultimately provides fulfillment.

We must rest in the knowledge that God is fixing certain things in our lives so we can be ready to be the person He called us to be. He wants to release His power through us in every circumstance and His power is always perfect in our weakness. The apostle Paul knew this when he stated:

> *And He said to me, "My grace is sufficient for you, for My strength is made perfect in weakness." Therefore most gladly I will rather boast in my infirmities, that the power of Christ may rest upon me* (2 Corinthians 12:9).

So for the rest of this study, let's name this God-directed journey, "The Wilderness." For most of us, the term "wilderness" produces negative mental pictures and brings out a wide range of emotions and questions, such as: How is a place of nothing going to make me stronger? As a fleshly creature, we only see a place that is void of hope, vision, and provision. For the ordinary, untrained man, the chances of survival, rescue, and recovery are slim.

Yet it is imperative that we approach this wilderness picture from a different perspective. As I mentioned before, most of us would rather journey in some paradise-like setting, for much of modern religion has only taught us about a God of prosperity. It is rare to hear a sermon about a God who molds His children by fire and adversity. Naturally, it will be a challenge for many to see the wilderness as a positive experience. Religion and false teachers have promulgated an idea that we are only to be concerned with getting blessed and receiving good things from the Lord. However, when troubles and storms come our way, our immediate response is to be fearful and complain. So are we really that different from the first generation of free Hebrews?

We must rest in the knowledge that God is fixing certain things in our lives so we can be ready to be the person He called us to be.

The wilderness experience is also an experience of isolation, where you may literally be left alone, perhaps abandoned by your earthly friends and companions. Instead of being angry and wondering why you are being shunned, it is a perfect opportunity to view this "space" as your extended quiet time with the Lord. God knows exactly where you are. He is also aware that you are part of a physical community needing to interact while at the same time reflecting upon the Israelite's experience as a means of understanding that He is working to get your attention.

In tandem with personal isolation, you may find that people have deserted you or purposely separated themselves. You may feel as if you're not going anywhere or that your life is stuck in some similar place. With that, you may feel as if you're not accomplishing anything. You also may feel like this because you may have no direct involvement with anything. The bright side to all this is that your wilderness is only for a season. He is testing you to see what really sustains your life: are works for God the things that will sustain your relationship with Him or is it God alone who sustains your spiritual life?

God does not intend for you to live the rest of your life in the wilderness. It is only when God wants to move you up in life or ministry that He tests you in the wilderness. As always, you need to remember that this is just for a season or a short period of life. Through this short period, God wants to find out if you are ready to do what He has called you to do. This is why you need to have a right heart and proper attitude. When God is testing you, He is looking for your response—how you will respond to Him.

The bright side to all this is that your wilderness is only for a season.

Our Response to the Wilderness

As you experience this extended season, your response will determine success or defeat. Attitude is the key and if you are teachable, you will humbly bring all that you are before God and lay it at His feet. You may think you are going to die; however, if you grumble, you are almost assured of repeating this season. Let not your heart grumble against God like the Israelites did when He brings you into the wilderness and your flesh questions Him.

> *For you have brought us out into this wilderness to kill this whole assembly with hunger* (Exodus 16:3).

> *Why is it you have brought us up out of Egypt, to kill us and our children and our livestock with thirst?* (Exodus 17:3).

The Israelites did not truly understand the purpose of why God had brought them to the desert. It was a time of preparation and an opportunity for them to learn of His true greatness. He wanted to show them that it was not a place to die, but a time to experience the supernatural power of God. It was a time where God wanted to demonstrate that He alone reigns supreme.

Have you been complaining like the Israelites about your wilderness experience? Do you feel as if you're about to die or that this process is leading you to nowhere? Are you grumbling? Are you frustrated and discouraged to the point where everything seems meaningless? Do you want out of your wilderness experience? If you answered "yes" to any of these questions, then your attitude and heart are mismatched. With this attitude it will not take long to fail. God wants you to have hope as you experience these things. He wants you to believe and trust in Him that He is about to do something fantastic in your life.

There are, of course, two ways that you can respond to God's training plan; you can obey or disobey. Disobedience will lead to an experience of frustration, resentment, and anger. If you disobey God, then you are going to stay in the wilderness and will never get to leave. Have you not experienced those individuals whose very spirit appears to have been left in the wilderness? You see them as bitter, angry, disappointed, and frustrated individuals walking around with a distinct "chip on their shoulder," lashing out and condemning everything around them. Yet they sit in the same pews that you do and faithfully come to church.

Have you been complaining like the Israelites about your wilderness experience?

Scripture clearly shows how that first generation of Israelites constantly disobeyed God and demonstrated a stiff-necked attitude toward the entire liberation experience.

> *So the Lord's anger was aroused against Israel, and He made them wander in the wilderness forty years, until all the generation that had done evil in the sight of the Lord was gone* (Numbers 32:13).

However, if you obey, God will lead you across the Jordan River and into the promise He has for you.

> *You shall diligently keep the commandments of the Lord your God, His testimonies, and His statutes which He has commanded you. And you shall do what is right*

> *and good in the sight of the Lord, that it may be well with you, and that you may go in and possess the good land of which the Lord swore to your fathers* (Deuteronomy 6:17-18).

Two questions about obedience are these: "Do you demonstrate faith when you obey?" and "Will your faith follow your obedience?" What the Lord Jesus is looking for is faith on the earth, just as God was looking for a nation-state that would be completely devoted to Him.

> *Nevertheless, when the Son of Man comes, will He really find faith on the earth?* (Luke 18:8).

God wants you to put all your trust in Him and wants you to know that He will provide for you. He promised that He will supply all of your needs in the wilderness and that you don't need to worry about anything.

Our Identity and Dependence Upon God

The experience of the wilderness is a time when you learn who you are in Christ and ultimately become grounded in your identity as His servant. This period is designed to show that your foundation is not based upon social order, but rather as His child and that your identity flows from this understanding. Unlike man who chooses to list accomplishments as a manner of recognition, God is pleased with you before you accomplish anything. Do not get the idea that God is more pleased with you when you do extraordinary things for Him. You need to know that He is pleased with you and He identifies you as His child first and foremost. This comes by being in relationship with Him.

> *Then a voice came from heaven, You are My beloved Son, in whom I am well pleased* (Mark 1:11).

God was well pleased with Jesus before He did anything for Him. God was pleased with Him because He was His own Son. God is well pleased with you also because you are His child.

The wilderness is also a time where God teaches you that you need to depend on Him for all your necessities as the ultimate provider. You depend on many things in the world to help you, such as intelligence, wealth, talent, position, etc. These are not necessarily bad, but God wants to train you to be totally dependent on Him. He does not want you to seek fleshly answers to your problems, but to understand the spiritual significance or meaning of them. He wants you to know that you can come to Him as the first solution to your problems. He wants you to become an overcomer, as loving parents do when they see their children battling new challenges.

> *For whatever is born of God overcomes the world. And this is the victory that has overcome the world—our faith* (1 John 5:4).

The apostle John's passage clearly shows that you can overcome any situation in your life. Since you have God's DNA within you, you have the ability to defeat all the adversity in your life. God is just waiting for you to come to Him before you try to solve your own problems through other means.

There is another perspective on the wilderness experience I would like to share. So far, your wilderness experience may have been focused on emptiness or isolation as a key outcome. Yet, perhaps your wilderness is a place of paradox. Instead of an austere experience, it is very possible you are walking in an existence of overwhelming busyness complemented by frantic scheduling, carpools, soccer matches, and overpowering work responsibilities, leaving you surrounded, isolated, and cut off.

Since you have God's DNA within you, you have the ability to defeat all the adversity in your life.

Yet the answer to the madness surrounding you is to seek God as your only source of strength.

For the joy of the Lord is your strength (Nehemiah 8:10).

He gives power to the weak and to those who have no might He increases strength. Even the youths shall faint and be weary and the young men shall utterly fall. But those who wait on the Lord shall renew their strength. They shall mount up with wings like eagles, they shall run and not be weary, they shall walk and not faint (Isaiah 40:29-31).

All too often, we move forward with intentions of asking God, but conveniently place Him as Plan B, or come to Him when things don't appear to be working out. Once again, the purpose of the wilderness is for us to learn to depend upon Him. The wilderness is filled with emptiness or may be overwhelming, but either way all of the answers are within our relationship to Him. He wants us to learn the importance of depending upon Him and the blessings that follow.

Tools for Wilderness Survival

In 1986, God told me to fast for 40 days. This was a long-term fast that the Lord was asking me to do. The only long-term fast I had experienced was for seven days. However, I obeyed and went up a prayer mountain to fast. I went from late October until one week before Christmas. About the thirty-third day of my fast, I wanted to quit because it was so difficult for me to handle. Then all of a sudden as I was reading the Book of Matthew, I came to the passage where it was talking about the Last Supper that Jesus had with His disciples. As I was reading that, suddenly hands marked with nails came out of the Bible. It was as if I was having communion with the Lord. As I was having this communion, I felt strength returning to my body. God strengthened me through this communion to finish my fast. I did not have any hunger during my fast after this encounter.

Three days after my fast at two in the morning, my room was covered with His glory. It was awesome, but terrifying at the same time. It is hard to explain how the atmosphere was. When God's glory is in a place, it is indescribable. While my room was covered with His glory, I had a vision of the Lord and two archangels. The Lord had a crown of thorns on his head yet there was no blood. He spoke about the significance of the crown of thorns. He said that I will face persecution and suffering but I will go through it with peace. He spoke to me on what will happen to me in the future.

This example shows how God calls us to depend upon Him and if we don't rely upon God, we will fail in the wilderness and in Christian ministry. Nobody will be able to successfully minister if they do not learn how to depend upon God. It is a discipline that needs to be taught and learned among the Christian community. People struggle with this issue throughout their whole life. God says to seek Him first and all that we need will be given to us.

When God's glory is in a place, it is indescribable.

But seek first the kingdom of God and His righteousness, and all these things shall be added to you. Therefore do not worry about tomorrow, for tomorrow will worry about its own things. Sufficient for the day is its own trouble (Matthew 6:33-34).

Many know and are familiar with this verse but not many actually believe it. Our dependence is found only in Him. People who don't believe in the Lord always worry about a multitude of things. They do multiple things to meet their needs. I see the same thing being done among Christians, too. With that attitude, how can we bring people to the Lord and help them to believe that God will take care of them when Christians themselves do not believe in this truth.

Due to this many people want to be independent. They want to do things their own way, and if trouble comes, they seek God out of desperation. This is not what God intended in life. That is why He brings us through the wilderness to let us know that we will not be able to make it unless we depend totally upon Him. Many people put their dependence on psychics, fortune tellers, and even prophecies. People want to have tangible things they can hold onto because it is something they can work with. In the wilderness, the only tangible thing we can hold onto is God. The wilderness is a place where we cannot help but depend only upon Him. It is to strengthen our relationship and fellowship with Him. He designed it that way to see how devoted His people will be to His Words and promises.

We need to put our failures aside and not let them take control of our lives.

One reason why it may be hard for us to depend on God is because we depended on men and they failed us. We may have had experiences where we were let down or people couldn't be trusted. We experience many failures in life. We can view failures not as opportunities to grow but as a lack of success. We might have felt betrayed by our failures or even people. Sometimes our past failures prevent us from trusting anything or anyone again. God wants us to put all that aside. He wants us to know that our past failures do not dictate our future. We need to put our failures aside and not let them take control of our lives.

THE WILDERNESS CHURCH AS AN EXAMPLE

First Corinthians 10:1-11 describes the Wilderness Church. These are the Israelites who came out of Egypt, crossed the Red Sea, and went through the wilderness. Paul writes to the church in Corinth and explains to them that the Israelites are an example of what not to do. He warns them not to follow the ways of the Israelites when they were in the wilderness. Many times God questioned the Israelites about their unbelief. He wanted to know if they were committed only to Him. God wanted their allegiance to be with Him and not man-made idols. God does not want us to repeat the same mistakes as the Israelites. History does not need to repeat itself.

> *As a dog returns to his own vomit, so a fool repeats his folly* (Proverbs 26:11).

You need to learn from your past mistakes and not repeat them. The Israelites, however, never learned from their mistakes. You read in the Bible how the Israelites went before the Lord when they were in trouble with prayers of desperation. After the Lord defeated their enemy, they went back and worshiped other idols. Later on when they were in trouble again, they prayed with desperation and the Lord delivered them once again. Mistakes like these need to be learned from and never repeated.

As you live your life, you are faced with various trials and obstacles. You cannot avoid them. All these things are inevitable, but you will be able to overcome each of them. These are the times that you need to live with a proper attitude. If you continue complaining and never seeing things through God's eyes, you will be like the Israelites. You will turn your backs against God and find other solutions.

If you continue complaining and never seeing things through God's eyes, you will be like the Israelites.

The Necessity of the Wilderness

I mentioned before how people will try to avoid the wilderness journey. If you do this, you will not experience the power of God in your life. You need to experience the wilderness to know what the power of God is and how you can activate it in your life. This is a time when God wants to change your mentality about the way you live. It is a time of transition. Everyone needs to go through times of transition. God wants to transition you from living in the flesh to living in the spirit.

The Transition in My Life

In the spring of 1985, I was praying in the sanctuary of my church, reflecting upon one of my assignments to lead discipleship training. As I knelt and meditated upon Psalms 1 through 18, the Lord spoke to me and directed my attention to Acts 1:1-8. Suddenly, the Holy Spirit stopped me and I saw an open vision concerning verse 8 where Luke comments, "But you shall receive power when the Holy Spirit has come upon you; and you shall be witnesses to Me in Jerusalem and in all

Judea and Samaria and to the end of the earth" (Acts 1:8). As the Word came into my heart, I saw a vision where Heaven was opened, fire came down from the throne of God, and I was baptized by it.

As the Word came into my heart, I saw a vision where Heaven was opened, fire came down from the throne of God, and I was baptized by it.

After the vision I was "slain in the spirit" and collapsed upon the floor. I did not know how long I remained in this state, but when I awoke I felt a new sense of boldness. The Lord reminded me of my life as a teenager attending junior high school in South Korea. As memories of my youth from the 1960s passed before me, I remembered attending church for the first time and the cold winter associated with that experience. My first trip to the house of God was with a friend whom I considered as close as a natural brother. My friend and his family were extraordinarily special. As my elder, I treated him with the respect of an older brother. His mother and father were devoted Christians and like second parents. They always encouraged me to attend church with them whenever I visited their home.

My first visit to their church was very unique. I did not understand any of the proceedings. Unlike at Western church sanctuaries, attendees in Korean churches sit on an open wooden floor. By the time I arrived, the church was filled.

Little did I know that a revival was underway so finding a place to sit was not easy. We found room in the back amongst floor cushions. I heard the pastor telling everyone in the church to pray in unison but I did not understand the language. As a first-time attendee, I did not know how to pray and I remained seated next to my friend's mother. Now I understand that the congregation was praying in tongues.

Suddenly, the pastor came down from the pulpit and began walking through the crowd of at least 250. He passed those in the front and advanced directly toward me. He stopped and laid his hands upon me and began praying over me. I remember the experience very clearly since the pastor was very tall and his hands were very large. I did not understand what he was saying or praying, but I do remember the physical manifestations when his fingers touched me. Even though it was in winter, my body became very hot and soon my underclothing was soaked in sweat. There was a distinct and actual presence and something did happen as a result of his prayers. As my vision continued, I was reminded by God that even though I was still in junior high school and had only attended church for the first time, He had touched me as a teenager for a very special reason.

After I received this fiery baptism, God led me to pray for the sick.

After I received this fiery baptism, God led me to pray for the sick. I prayed for cancer patients and people in the Intensive

Care Unit (ICU) and other parts of the hospital. Soon many signs, wonders, miracles, and healings took place. The Lord guided me step-by-step and showed me how He was going to use me.

The Vision of My Calling

Within a year, in 1986, I began wrestling with the Lord Jesus Christ each evening for three months. During the three months, Jesus visited me every night in a vision. He said that He called me to be a minister. After hearing that I refused to accept that calling. I continued refusing until finally at the end of three months, I gave up and accepted the call. During these periods, the Lord showed me a vision of how He planned to use me in creative ways. He showed me that the lame would walk and those with polio would be healed, along with many other signs and wonders. In the spring of 1986, God reaffirmed my calling in a very special way through a spectacular vision.

The Lord took me in the Spirit and showed me a massive football field and sports coliseum. Assembled within the stadium were more than 100,000 people and overflow auditoriums were filled as well. As I approached the pulpit and overlooked the crowd, I could see this was not a typical Christian gathering but rather a massive evangelistic meeting for the lost. Those who were gathered at the meeting before me had striking appearances, as they were covered in black from head to toe. It looked as if death had cloaked each one. As I began to preach the Lord's message, an amazing transformation began to take place. Those whose bodies were covered in black began to change, and they became white as if they were cleansed by the purest snow. God began restoring the lost limbs of those with deformed extremities. In addition, those with missing eyes received new eyes and many other signs and wonders followed.

During this vision, I did not lay my hands on anyone because the glory of God was totally manifested and people were soaking in it. The Lord spoke to me and said, "What you are supernaturally witnessing will take place in the ministry I have placed upon you." God was transitioning me to a lifestyle of living in the Spirit.

Renewing Your Mind

Just as the Israelites were filled with Egyptian knowledge and mindsets, much of what makes up your understanding derived from man. With this information, you almost always rationalize your situations and calculate formulas on how you can overcome obstacles. In order for your mind to be renewed by God, you must be willing to let go and allow Him to refresh every part of you. As Paul states in Romans 12:1-2:

> *I beseech you therefore, brethren, by the mercies of God, that you present your bodies a living sacrifice, holy, acceptable to God, which is your reasonable service. And do not be conformed to this world, but be transformed by the renewing of your mind, that you may prove what is that good and acceptable and perfect will of God.*

Much of what you retain in your mind is potentially useless and unnecessary. I believe God is seeking to filter out the excess and have you focus on the necessary things. In a sense, living for Him and His Word becomes a filtering mechanism that ultimately develops a Christian world view. You need to crucify all those ideas that have been absorbed in your life and prevent you from approaching the Cross with boldness. You need to make the Word of God the standard for living, and its contents need to rise above all other secular knowledge and information.

The Making of a True Instrument of God

Another reason why you need the wilderness experience is because God wants to make you a true instrument that He can use for His Kingdom. He wants to transform you so that you can be an instrument for His glory. There is always a purpose why God does things the way He does. Your mind is not capable of fully understanding how God works. You just need to obey what He says in your life. I can see this principle at work in my own life.

My Last Experience of a 40-Day Fast

On my last extended fast, God asked me to fast for 40 days without water. I asked the Lord, "How can a man survive without water for 40 days?" His response was, "Did my son Moses drink water for 40 days?" During the first week of the fast, I rebelled and drank water. However, after a week, I noticed red dots appearing on my skin that did not itch. I asked God, "What is this?" His reply was, "You did not obey Me." After that, I knew what He meant and so I repented and obeyed His command for the next 33 days. During the remaining month, God's presence covered me. I had amazing strength, for even though I was only sleeping four hours per day, He was training me eight hours per day with prayer and study of the Word. Yet in spite of no food or water, I only lost 28 pounds. Without this experience, I believe I would not be a true instrument of God today.

All Christians need to go through their own personal wilderness.

All Christians need to go through their own personal wilderness. This is especially true for those who are called into the ministry. You should not be alarmed when the wilderness season begins. Instead, you need to rejoice and see how God wants to train you to be an instrument. That is why His Spirit leads you to places that you do not want to be. Since you do not want to be in those places, you try to run away or avoid going through them. This is why you need to know the true purpose of the wilderness.

> *For I know the thoughts that I think toward you, says the Lord, thoughts of peace and not of evil, to give you a future and a hope* (Jeremiah 29:11).

God wants to make you into a vessel that He can use for His glory. He has given you a future to look forward to. This is the hope He wants residing in your life. He also created you for the purpose that you would glorify Him. The way you glorify God is by fulfilling what He has called you to do.

Everyone who is called by My name, whom I have created for My glory; I have formed him, yes, I have made him (Isaiah 43:7).

God does not just give His glory to anyone; it is given to those who are His own. Once you are filled with His glory, you can be the resource for this world. God wants to manifest His glory through your life. In order for this to occur, you need to embrace your wilderness experience. You need to embrace it with a proper attitude. You need to accept the idea that God knows what He is doing. He knows why you need the wilderness and how it will change you from just being ordinary Christians into extraordinary followers of Him.

God Supplies All of Your Needs

God always knows exactly what you need. God supplies all of your needs in the wilderness, not only materialistic things. When we observe the reactions of the Israelites, we see they were consistently dissatisfied with the food God gave them. God wanted to give them spiritual food but their desire was always set on the pleasures of Egypt. They started to complain and question God. The Israelites missed the point on what God wanted to teach them. He wanted them to know that His blessings were far beyond what they had in Egypt. But the Israelites did not prosper because they denied the living Rock.

Far too many Christians have the same attitude and mindset. You may expect God to meet your needs in a certain way, but God works differently. He knows exactly what is needed in your life. God will meet your needs, but it will come in ways that you least expect. The need that He wants to supply is completely molding and making you into a holy vessel as His instrument. Jesus is teaching you the mature Christian life in the fullness of the Spirit. There are always things inside of you that need to be changed. The need God is supplying is total dependence upon Him. He does not want you to worry about things, doubt His promises, or lose faith or hope. What God is supplying is the completion of your character and identity in Christ.

He does not want you to worry about things, doubt His promises, or lose faith or hope.

In the wilderness, you are being exposed to many opportunities to learn the ways of the Lord. Once you become a mature Christian living in the fullness of the Spirit, then the physical things you need will come. Patience is critical. Instead of chasing after these things, you need to become a God chaser.

> *But seek first the kingdom of God and His righteousness, and all these things shall be added to you* (Matthew 6:33).

We are all familiar with Matthew 6:33. This is our first priority. This is God's promise to us that all physical needs will be met. God is showing us what the most important need is in our lives.

When was the last time you were dependent upon God? Is God your first priority every day? Do you need Him more than other things? Your biggest need is to have the fullness of God residing in you. You may be looking to satisfy your physical needs, but God is looking to satisfy your spiritual needs first. Because you are made in the image of God, you can live by the Spirit of God.

Points to Ponder

1. Are you experiencing anything similar to the first generation of free Hebrews?

2. Does it seem like God is taking decades to lead you toward your destiny?

3. Are you on the verge of hardening your heart due to what you perceive as lack of progress or fulfillment?

Chapter 4

The Way of Holiness

THE PURPOSE OF THE WILDERNESS

IN the following chapters I will examine God's purpose for establishing the wilderness so you can view this opportunity as a season of increased faith and strength. As the Lord states in Isaiah 35:1-10:

> *The wilderness and the wasteland shall be glad for them. And the desert shall rejoice and blossom as the rose. Even with joy and singing. The glory of Lebanon shall be given to it. The excellence of Carmel and Sharon. They shall see the glory of the Lord. The excellency of our God.*
>
> *Strengthen the weak hands and make firm the feeble knees. Say to those who are fearful-hearted, "Be strong,*

do not fear! Behold, your God will come with vengeance, with the recompense of God; He will come and save you."

Then the eyes of the blind shall be opened and the ears of the deaf shall be unstopped. Then the lame shall leap like a deer and the tongue of the dumb sing. For waters shall burst forth in the wilderness and streams in the desert. The parched ground shall become a pool and the thirsty land springs of water; in the habitation of jackals, where each lay, there shall be grass with reeds and rushes.

A highway shall be there and a road. And it shall be called the Highway of Holiness. The unclean shall not pass over it but it shall be for others. Whoever walks the road, although a fool, shall not go astray. No lion shall be there, nor shall any ravenous beast go up on it; it shall not be found there. But the redeemed shall walk there and the ransomed of the Lord shall return and come to Zion with singing, with everlasting joy on their heads. They shall obtain joy and gladness and sorrow and sighing shall flee away.

A) Restoration of the Kingdom

Strengthen the weak hands, and make firm the feeble knees (Isaiah 35:3).

We must understand that God's ultimate plan is for the full restoration of His Kingdom. When it is restored, joyfulness will reign and God's strength will be released, liberating His people from fear.

It was Isaiah who understood the ramifications and vision behind a restored Kingdom of God. Therefore if you are to fully appreciate it, you must closely examine some key verses to gain a greater understanding of this promise. Isaiah tells us that restoration will bring meaningful change to God's people, and as a result, they will be filled with wisdom and knowledge that blossoms like a rose. He further emphasizes that the emptiness inside will be replaced with joy and we will witness healing and miracles. It is this visual symbolism of God's power that brings such comfort. In addition, we will observe bursting waters, which symbolize life and the flow of anointing through His people. When this anointing flows, then all the healings and miracles will take place.

> *And he showed me a pure river of water of life, clear as crystal, proceeding from the throne of God and of the Lamb. In the middle of its street, and on either side of the river, was the tree of life, which bore twelve fruits, each tree yielding its fruit every month. The leaves of the tree were for the healing of the nations* (Revelation 22:1-2).

Protected by the Blood

As God's people we need to remember the guiding principle behind God's power, which is, when we accept His rule, the enemy cannot stand in His presence. Instead of fearing the enemy, we need to believe it is the enemy who fears us.

> *No weapon formed against you shall prosper* (Isaiah 54:17).

There is no power or weapon that can prevail, nor will any spell, curse, or magic incantation be successful because we are covered by the blood of Jesus that was shed for us on Calvary.

Just as the Israelites could watch a pillar of fire by night and a smoke cloud by day, we have the Cross to constantly remind us of His power.

If we fear the enemy, we provide an open door. Just as the Israelites abandoned God after His mighty works in the Egyptian desert, we can be susceptible to forgetting Him as well. So we must remember that just as the Israelites could watch a pillar of fire by night and a smoke cloud by day, we have the Cross to constantly remind us of His power. His sacrifice is the assured destruction of our enemies and our old life.

> *Therefore, if anyone is in Christ, he is a new creation; old things have passed away; behold, all things have become new* (2 Corinthians 5:17).

B) Restoration of Joy and Healing

The only way that we can release the power and authority in our lives is through joy. Joy is the key ingredient to strengthening ourselves in the wilderness. Yet joy comes as a by-product, or is the end-state, of our emotions. If it was simply easy to get it, our world would be a much different place. So then how do we receive such supernatural joy?

It is through a process known as being filled with the Spirit of God.

> *He who believes in Me, as the Scripture has said, out of his heart will flow rivers of living water* (John 7:38).

It is this infilling that permits living water to flow and results in joy beyond human understanding. Without this precious end-state, we are dry and appear to be passionless and without focus. Yet blessings of this type are almost forgotten by most of modern Christianity. As His children, we must realize that God has never stopped operating from this paradigm. He wants us to be filled with joyous passion because without it, it will be impossible to leave the wilderness and cross our Jordan River.

It is from joy that God wants to take us to places of better pasture.

It is from joy that God wants to take us to places of better pasture. When we are in these fields of green, we will experience abundance because intimacy has been reestablished so that we can shout for joy and sing.

> *In Your presence is fullness of joy* (Psalm 16:11).

When God restores the Garden of Eden in our lives, joy and gladness will follow and from here we will have the power and authority restored to us. Without joy, we will lose our passion, desire, and hunger for God. We need to be constantly filled with joy because it is the driving force that increases our passion for the Lord. We need to be excited because God has given us a future and a new direction.

Praise and Worship

> *For the Lord will comfort Zion. He will comfort all her waste places; He will make her wilderness like Eden, and her desert like the garden of the Lord; Joy and gladness will be found in it, thanksgiving and the voice of melody* (Isaiah 51:3).

Strong defines what joy, gladness, thanksgiving, and a voice of melody means for us today. *Joy* represents "rejoicing, exultation." *Gladness* represents "being cheerful, a happy issue." *Thanksgiving* represents "a confession, giving praise to God, a thank offering, a sacrifice of thanksgiving, thanksgiving in song." *A voice of melody* represents "singing forth praises, to make music accompanied by the voice, hence to celebrate in song and music, a musical piece or song to be accompanied by an instrument." (These are all taken from Strong Number OT 2172, OT 6963). In summation, all of these characteristics of joy lead us to a place where our heart will be overflowing with passion for God.

As with the architectural design of the Tabernacle and Temple of Israel, we still find ourselves moving in a progression from the gates toward the Holy of Holies, which represents personal intimacy with God. As modern believers or priests, we must deliberately enter His presence in praise and worship.

> *Therefore by Him let us continually offer the sacrifice of praise to God, that is, the fruit of our lips, giving thanks to His name* (Hebrews 13:15).

THE TRUE MEANING OF WORSHIP

Modern believers need to know the full meaning of worshiping God, because it is rarely exercised in post-modern Christianity. Many leaders believe these moments have passed away or have been sealed, and worse yet, many ignore them when these moments do come. Therefore, we cannot count churches to lead the way in this area. We must realize that God will not be limited to a literal temple or synagogue as we communicate through the Spirit, and that learning to worship outside these confines is critical to achieving the joy and intimacy we seek with Him.

We need to cleanse ourselves of fleshly thoughts so that our spirits can worship God by His Spirit.

The first thing before entering God's presence is to conduct a spiritual inventory and preparation of our body, mind, and heart. This means that we need to cleanse ourselves of fleshly thoughts so that our spirit can worship God by His Spirit. Basically we must be humble enough to rid ourselves of everything that will hinder us from worshiping Him with our entire heart, soul, mind, and spirit.

> *But the hour is coming, and now is, when the true worshipers will worship the Father in spirit and truth; for the Father is seeking such to worship Him. God is Spirit, and those who worship Him must worship in spirit and truth* (John 4:23-24).

To worship God "in spirit" means to worship from our whole heart. It also means to worship by the power of the Holy Spirit. To worship "in truth" means to not conceal or hold back anything from Him.

> *The spirit of a man is the lamp of the Lord, searching all the inner depths of his heart* (Proverbs 20:27).

> *However, when He, the Spirit of truth, has come, He will guide you into all truth; for He will not speak on His own authority but whatever He hears He will speak; and He will tell you things to come* (John 16:13).

We also must allow all of our human nature (pride) to be destroyed by the Holy Spirit. We must have the fire of the Holy Spirit and when we receive it, then the work of the Son, the Anointed One, can be manifested through us and God will be glorified. We must be in one spirit with Jesus.

> *But he who is joined to the Lord is one spirit with Him* (1 Corinthians 6:17).

There are no special skills or talents necessary to worship. If anything, all that is needed is a hunger to focus upon

God. We need to focus only on His presence and release our concerns about others and their ideas. After all, that is why it is termed a personal relationship. This is something that will only be between us and God. That is why praise and worship is not just about singing songs or going through a routine on Sundays.

Through praise and worship, healing and deliverance is manifested. Isaiah 35:7 describes that deliverance will take place and satanic and demonic power will be cast away.

> *The parched ground shall become a pool and the thirsty land springs of water; in the habitation of jackals, where each lay, there shall be grass with reeds and rushes.*

The "habitation of jackals" refers to the influence of the devil. Through praise and worship, satanic and demonic powers are cast out and life is given.

Intimacy With God

God wants to restore intimacy with His people and create an atmosphere where this astonishing closeness can be experienced. However, we need to be reminded how to enter in and experience this supernatural gift.

How we, as His children, choose to enter our Father's gates is of utmost importance. Our personal procession cannot be with an attitude of ungratefulness, because the first song that we sing upon entering His gates will be of thanksgiving from our hearts. As we pass through these gates and into the courtyard, we are instructed to praise God. We do this by singing joyfully, clapping, dancing, and raising our hands: all of these demonstrate our heartfelt thanksgiving to Him.

The first song that we sing upon entering His gates will be of thanksgiving from our hearts.

As we continue celebrating the Lord, we are drawn from the courtyard into the inner courts or Holy Place. It is a moment when our awareness of Him surpasses the cares and worries of our carnal flesh and we commune with Him in reverence, hands raised above our head, literally being overwhelmed. Then, without realizing it, we find ourselves in a moment that defies description and the anointing and power of God takes over.

We can expect that our human body will simply be too frail to do anything but bow down or lay prostrate before God. Many people call this "being slain in the Spirit" or "pressing in" as a component of the total surrender necessary to be totally intimate with Him. Once we have entered, we must be wise enough to linger or tarry in these moments. It is here that our spirits yield to His and we are formed in His image and begin to reflect the image of His Son, Jesus Christ.

Through praise, our hearts and lives can be transformed. The lifestyle of praise changes attitudes and allows bountiful seeds to be planted in the formerly fallow ground of our hearts. Sadly, very few believers have experienced this level of intimacy with God. There has been little instruction on how to prepare ourselves, how to enter in, and a genuine belief in the supernatural. However, God desires His Bride to draw closer and if we are to be fulfilled, we need to praise Him daily.

I am convinced that failing to really know Him on a Holy of Holies level is one of the root problems associated with post-modern Christianity. This is why many leave church unfulfilled. They leave without experiencing an intimacy and find the inside of the church as dry and legalistic as the world outside. For most people, attending church is no more exciting than any other "chore" during the week and it is done to avoid issues rather than solve them. Many people believe that as long as they keep the Sabbath day, attend church, and act responsibly, then they are doing fine. However, that is simply not the case with a God who has an incredible gift to share.

Leaders must model a lifestyle of giving thanks and praise.

God is rekindling the love of the people toward Him through praise and worship. He wants to restore passion in people's hearts for His Kingdom. Therefore, leaders must model a lifestyle of giving thanks and praise. God called everyone to be a high priest in His house. No matter what the situation or circumstance, we must enter into His gates with thanksgiving and into His courts with praise (see Ps. 100:4).

Therefore I challenge you to enter His gates and courtyard with vibrant singing, accompanied by clapping hands, dancing, and a variety of instruments. This will help people experience the meaning of true worship as they kneel in an act of surrendering with their hands raised to God. The people in the church are no longer being entertained by a choir or by some vocalists, but are experiencing the anointing of God in a fresh new way. Through this, God provides the motivation and fire needed so that we can go and love the world.

> *On that day I will raise up the tabernacle of David, which has fallen down, and repair its damages; I will raise up its ruins, and rebuild it as in the days of old; that they may possess the remnant of Edom, and all the Gentiles who are called by My name, says the Lord who does this thing* (Amos 9:11-12).

Healing

> *He will come and save you. Then the eyes of the blind shall be opened, and the ears of the deaf shall be unstopped. Then the lame shall leap like a deer, and the tongue of the dumb sing. For waters shall burst forth in the wilderness, and streams in the desert. The parched ground shall become a pool, and the thirsty land springs of water* (Isaiah 35:4-7).

We read from this Scripture that another gift of God is healing in our lives. When Jesus died for our sins, not only were our sins forgiven but we were also healed from all our sicknesses and diseases.

> *Bless the Lord, O my soul; And all that is within me, bless His holy name! Bless the Lord, O my soul, and forget not all His benefits; Who forgives all your iniquities,*

Who heals all your diseases (Psalm 103:1-3).

Surely He has borne our griefs and carried our sorrows; Yet we esteemed Him stricken, smitten by God, and afflicted. But He was wounded for our transgressions, He was bruised for our iniquities; the chastisement for our peace was upon Him, and by His stripes we are healed (Isaiah 53:4-5).

Who Himself bore our sins in His own body on the tree, that we, having died to sins, might live for righteousness—by whose stripes you were healed (1 Peter 2:24).

The Bible states that all of our sicknesses and diseases are healed by the stripes of Jesus. God's words are promises in our lives, and we should expect them to manifest.

Deliverance

The devil has caused the ills and sorrows of humankind since the Garden of Eden to the present. His desire to be equal to God will continue until he is finally cast down into the lake of fire. Even though he may be roaming around the world, we are still delivered from his control. God has promised deliverance, and even if we are oppressed, God promised rest for His people. Since God disarmed all our enemies at the Cross, we can be sure of deliverance in our lives. I will explain in more detail in the chapter on spiritual warfare.

Living Water

And He showed me a pure river of water of life, clear as crystal, proceeding from the throne of God and of the Lamb (Revelation 22:1).

How can we have living water flow out of our lives? When we get strength from God, living waters will burst forth. The living water that we have needs to flow so that people will have an opportunity to experience His awesome presence. Being joyful is the key to releasing this living water.

He who believes in Me, as the Scripture has said, out of his heart will flow rivers of living water (John 7:38).

Way of Holiness

Once God releases His strength and living water flows inside of us, then no attack upon us will be successful because we are living in the way of holiness. When we are walking in the way of holiness, we are protected by God from all attacks of the enemy. He will not be able to harm us any longer, and this is the reason why everlasting joy will be upon our lives. Doesn't it feel good to hear that the enemy will not be able to attack us as long as we are walking in this path?

Points to Ponder

1. Have you received such supernatural joy through being filled with the Spirit of God? Why or why not?

2. Are you modeling a lifestyle of giving thanks and praise? If not, why not?

3. How can you have living water flow out of your life? Think of five ways and take action today.

Chapter 5

Highway to God

THUS far the motivation behind this truth has been to capture God's purpose for establishing the new wilderness. Yet in addition to this primary endeavor, I want to introduce another aspect known as becoming a highway for God. This idea revolves around the premise of being used as active guides and showing the lost and the prodigal a way back to Him. Perhaps your purpose will be to light the path, serve as guards, or be the humble sand which they tread upon. Yet regardless of the role, God is counting upon you to be a faithful and trusted servant. However, before you can be released to perform these tasks, you need to become suitable vessels that are sanctified and fully prepared to act as mature leaders through teaching and worship to be used for His glory. This is why your desert experience is necessary and serves as an integral component of a much larger requirement.

As part of this pathway or highway for God, you must be able to demonstrate that a relationship with Him is real and accessible. You need to be messengers of the glorious news that heralds the new covenant God established two thousand years ago at the moment of Jesus' death. At that very moment, the veil of separation that stood between you and God was supernaturally removed. It was this act, symbolized by the ripping of the curtain in the Jewish temple, which signaled all humankind, Jews and Gentiles, that a new enduring relationship and promise were in effect.

> *Therefore, brethren, having boldness to enter the Holiest by the blood of Jesus, by a new and living way which He consecrated for us, through the veil, that is, His flesh* (Hebrews 10:19-20).

> *"Comfort, yes, comfort My people!" says your God. "Speak comfort to Jerusalem and cry out to her. That her warfare is ended, that her iniquity is pardoned; For she has received from the Lord's hand double for all her sins." The voice of one crying in the wilderness: "Prepare the way of the Lord; Make straight in the desert a highway for our God. Every valley shall be exalted and every mountain and hill brought low; The crooked places shall be made straight and the rough places smooth; The glory of the Lord shall be revealed, and all flesh shall see it together; For the mouth of the Lord has spoken"* (Isaiah 40:1-5).

Sin Pardoned

It was the work upon Calvary that opened the way for forgiveness of sin and provides you the power and authority to wage spiritual warfare in the name of Jesus.

Let the saints be joyful in glory; Let them sing aloud on their beds. Let the high praises of God be in their mouth and a two-edged sword in their hand. To execute vengeance on the nations and punishments on the peoples; To bind their kings with chains and their nobles with fetters of iron; To execute on them the written judgment—This honor have all His saints. Praise the Lord! (Psalm 149:5-9)

The Glory of God

God wants you to be available so He can visit you at any time. Before you can reflect His glory, certain things need to be accomplished. Let me explain what your actions should be through these verses.

- "Every valley shall be exalted" means that every humble man will be exalted.

Humble yourselves in the sight of the Lord and He will lift you up (James 4:10).

- "Every mountain and hill brought low" means that every pride will be humbled.

For whoever exalts himself will be humbled, and he who humbles himself will be exalted (Luke 14:11).

- "The crooked places shall be made straight" means that if anything goes wrong, God wants to make it straight because He wants us to be a highway for Him. God desires to manifest His glory.

How will the glory of the Lord be revealed? It will come only when you become a highway for Him. The highway is the way of holiness.

A highway shall be there, and a road, and it shall be called the Highway of Holiness (Isaiah 35:8).

I mentioned this concept a few pages ago and described how you must allow God to develop you into a living example of selflessness. Therefore, if you are to obey Him, you must believe He will move in your life and acknowledge that people will begin to see and examine you from this perspective. In a sense, you become living resources for others and show them the path toward a real relationship with God.

Now it shall come to pass in the latter days that the mountain of the Lord's house shall be established on the top of the mountains and shall be exalted above the hills; and all nations shall flow to it. Many people shall come and say, "Come, and let us go up to the mountain of the Lord, to the house of the God of Jacob. He will teach us His ways, and we shall walk in His paths." For out of Zion shall go forth the law, and the word of the Lord from Jerusalem (Isaiah 2:2-3).

Christians need to confirm this purpose and be confident of it as well. You have been given the map and directions (Bible and Holy Spirit) for access to Jesus. Unfortunately, there are many who are prideful and do not believe that they need God.

However, once people observe His glory, their hearts will be humbled. That is why the Bible states that every mountain and hill will be brought low. It is saying that God will change people's hearts.

Living Beyond the Mundane

God also wants His people to know Him. He is personal and makes Himself available. He is not some far-off deity sitting in an ethereal palace reigning from a place of fear. He reveals His will and purposes to us and wants us to hear His voice. It is His heart's desire to communicate with us.

> *Surely I will pour out My spirit on you; I will make My words known to you* (Proverbs 1:23).

We need to hear God in the wilderness. He wants us to have the very life of God within us. The way we can hear the voice of God is if we are spiritually seated next to Him on the throne.

> *Incline your ear, and come to Me. Hear, and your soul shall live; and I will make an everlasting covenant with you—the sure mercies of David* (Isaiah 55:3).

When we are seated next to God, He is always speaking. This is why the Scripture states that if we do not listen to Him, our soul cannot thrive. In this present day, many claim to be Christians and attend church, yet they are not hearing God's voice. Instead, they operate within a paradigm of routine religion. They arrive on Sunday morning with a convenience store mentality where they expect to be "filled up" with minimal participation. There is certainly no expectancy in their heart to meet Jesus in a fresh, dynamic way.

This lukewarm persona is exactly the opposite of what God wants. He asks us to be patient and take the time to commune with Him. If we truly believe that He is the King of kings, then we will not be in such a rush to leave His house for Sunday football or soccer. Instead, this will be the most important day of the week and take its place as the capstone of a week spent seeking Him. It takes patience to hear and know Him and for many, patience is considered a luxury they do not have time for.

We need to stop and come to a peaceful halt to hear God's voice so we can be obedient.

Instead, we need to stop and come to a peaceful halt, literally working to hear God's voice so we can be obedient. We have to listen to what He is saying because the throne of God is already established in our heart. God promised that He would meet us at the mercy seat. Are we taking time to just stand still when we arrive? In addition, we must challenge ourselves by asking the following questions. "Are my practices demonstrating a lifestyle and highway for God?" "Are the things that I am doing bringing Him the glory and leading others into a more realistic relationship with Him?"

And there I will meet with you, and I will speak with you from above the mercy seat, from between the two cherubim which are on the ark of the Testimony, about everything which I will give you in commandment to the children of Israel (Exodus 25:22).

And you shall put it before the veil that is before the ark of the Testimony, before the mercy seat that is over the Testimony, where I will meet with you (Exodus 30:6).

I have been crucified with Christ; it is no longer I who live, but Christ lives in me; and the life which I now live in the flesh I live by faith in the Son of God, who loved me and gave Himself for me (Galatians 2:20).

When God reveals things, He is actually pouring Himself out. It is at the throne of God that we have an intimacy level through His personal revelation.

And he showed me a pure river of water of life, clear as crystal, proceeding from the throne of God and of the Lamb (Revelation 22:1).

There are many things attached to our lives that are from the world and we need to shake them off. The Bible teaches us that we are spiritually seated with Jesus in heavenly places.

And raised us up together, and made us sit together in the heavenly places in Christ Jesus (Ephesians 2:6).

Shake yourself from the dust, arise; Sit down, O Jerusalem! Loose yourself from the bonds of your neck, O captive daughter of Zion! (Isaiah 52:2).

The dust represents our fleshly life. Flesh has nothing to do with the Kingdom of God. You cannot live in the flesh if you want to hear God.

> *Now this I say, brethren, that flesh and blood cannot inherit the kingdom of God; nor does corruption inherit incorruption* (1 Corinthians 15:50).

Since your flesh will corrupt your spirit, you need to constantly be living in the Spirit. God communicates with you through His Spirit.

> *God is Spirit, and those who worship Him must worship in spirit and truth* (John 4:24).

God is Spirit and that is the only way we can communicate with Him. It is also at this place where the presence of God is in our midst. When God pours Himself out to us, He wants to consume us with His very presence. In His presence, there is power and strength. We need the very life of God to be manifested in us.

My Call to Minister in Japan

To better clarify the concept of becoming a highway for God, I feel compelled to share a series of testimonies regarding my call to minister in Japan. For those of you who are unaware, Japan is considered by mission experts to be an extraordinarily difficult field. At present, most of Japanese society is involved in a mixture of faith practices ranging from Buddhism to Shintoism, a nature-based religious practice. All Christian faiths combined account for less than two percent of the Japanese population.

Regardless of the statistics, I firmly believe that God has a plan for Japan and that His campaign of justice and freedom has begun. In December 1998, I went to Tokyo on a marketing research trip with one of my mission supporters who is the owner of a New York garment business. Although a far cry from my current profession and training, my secular academic work was in international business and marketing. Therefore, I saw this trip as a great opportunity.

I saw this trip as a great opportunity.

We departed Newark-Liberty International Airport in the evening and arrived in Narita, Japan around 11:20 A.M. the following day. After arriving, we commuted to Tokyo and conducted a series of business meetings. We checked into our hotel late that evening and immediately prepared for bed. It had been an absolutely exhausting period. The travel, the business meetings, and the time change were draining.

After an hour of sleep, the awesome presence of God filled my hotel room and the Lord stirred me, moving me to intercede for Japan. I began to pray and during the rest of the night, I was compelled to cry and weep. At around 8:30 in the morning, the Lord spoke to me and said, "I put this nation in your hand and Japan is ready to receive My power. I delegate you to release My power in this nation and raise Japanese-Christian and Christian business people to recover the economic problems in Japan." In addition, the Lord told me, "When Japan has recovered economically and financially, I will use that material blessing to reach Southeast Asia."

I wondered and asked the Lord, "Why just Southeast Asia?" The Lord then clearly explained that this level of blessing was necessary since Japan was responsible for terrible oppression before and during World War II. Yet instead of describing this as a punishment, the Lord said He was going to pay them back with His love. From that moment, I have found God opening doors for me to minister in Japanese-Christian churches.

Prior to this revelation at a leadership conference in the United States, I had another extraordinary vision with God that involved Dr. David Yonggi Cho, the founder of Yoido Full Gospel Church, located in the Republic of Korea. One of my friends was hosting this conference and invited my wife and me to attend. After the conference, the Lord showed me in a vision that Dr. Cho was looking for his successor and that there were four candidates. Three were over 55 and I was in my 40s.

After the conference, the Lord showed me in a vision that Dr. Cho was looking for his successor and that there were four candidates.

I shared this experience with my wife and told her I did not have any special relationship with Dr. Cho and therefore could not comprehend why the Lord gave me this vision. So we continued to pray and three years later, the Lord gave me a subsequent vision that again included Dr. Cho. During this second experience, a couple who attended Yoido Full Gospel and sang in their choir told me that Dr. Cho wished I would come to his office and accompany him on a home visit.

Although this request seemed strange, out of respect I embarked upon the journey. Upon arrival, Dr. Cho greeted me and took me to his car, a BMW 740. We then traveled to a large, modern-style home, where I observed a man who had been paralyzed for 50 years. His home reminded me of residences within the wealthiest parts of Tokyo, Japan. Of course, we understood that the purpose of our trip was to visit and pray, but interestingly enough Dr. Cho asked me to lead the prayer. "Why don't you lay your hands on him and pray?" Dr. Cho said. Since I respected this man of God, I obeyed. Instantly, the paralytic was healed and immediately rose up. Yet strangely, as soon as the man was upon his feet, Dr. Cho departed. I then noted that the man had been lying upon a traditional Japanese floor mat called "tatami." This vision was long and strange. I sought confirmation by asking one of the elders at Yoido Full Gospel what kind of automobile Dr. Cho drove, which they confirmed as being a BMW 740.

Then in 1998, I learned that Dr. Cho had chosen to suspend Yoido's mission efforts in Japan after 18 years of work. At first I did not understand the original vision, but then I began to recognize that God was moving and looking for a man that would carry on after Dr. Cho's departure. In the natural, it might appear as if a disaster was in the making; however in the supernatural, it might be described as a baton exchange between racers in a track and field event. Regardless, it was obvious that God was working in a special way and had no plans to withdraw from Japan.

In mid-1999, there was a Church Growth International (CGI) meeting in Yokohama, Japan. A week before my travel, I was praying at 4:30 A.M. and in another vision, I saw Dr. Cho and myself sitting next to each other talking on an airplane. In reality, I knew this would not be possible, since he usually flies first class. The next week, I flew to Korea, arriving at Gimpo airport very early in the morning. Since my connecting flight was not until 9:20 A.M., I took a shower and got ready early so I could speak immediately upon arriving in Japan.

As part of my preparation, I checked in early and was assigned a business class seat on the upper deck of a 747. About ten minutes before departure, I heard a lot of noise in the back. I turned my head to look and there appeared Dr. Cho with some people climbing the steps toward business class. I did not know the plane did not have a first class area. The first level was all economy seating and the upper deck was only business class. There was simply no first class seating available. Then Dr. Cho came and sat down across the aisle from me. After he settled, we greeted each other and he fell asleep.

There was no conversation, but I took this encounter as confirmation regarding my work in Japan.

I sat observing a man of God who was physically exhausted and tired. It was morning and we were on our way to Tokyo.

We never talked during the flight because he slept the entire flight. I recalled how God reminded me that we would fly together. When our flight arrived at Narita Airport, we greeted each other and went our separate ways. There was no conversation, but I took this encounter as confirmation regarding my work in Japan.

Japan and Korea

In 2002, I had another vision from the Lord. I was standing in an old, traditional church building that was terribly dark. Suddenly in the vision, I saw twin girls about two years old running toward me. Simultaneously, both of them jumped into my arms. However, I was only able to catch the girl on the left and the child on my right slipped to the floor. She immediately started crying and I bent down to soothe and comfort her. Then I put both of them in my arms and departed for the exit of the old church building. As soon as I opened the door, a very bright light representing the Glory of the Lord appeared.

The Lord spoke to me and said, "These girls are representative of apostolic churches. The child on the right represents a Korean apostolic church and the girl on the left represents a Japanese apostolic church." Furthermore, the Lord stated, "These two churches cannot be separated. These two nations will arise as true apostolic churches and will plant houses of worship all over the world." Since then, God has used me to work with churches in Japan, Korea, and now China as well. After this vision, the Lord laid it upon my heart to see the planting of an additional 3,000 Japanese churches during the next five years, adding to the 7,900 that currently exist. I believe that God will continue to work on this nation and use it for His glory.

Conclusion

When you are in the presence of God, He reveals His plans to you, for He wants His plan to be made known. When His plans are made known and fulfilled, then God's glory will be manifested. The Bible even states:

> *Surely the Lord God does nothing, unless He reveals His secret to His servants the prophets* (Amos 3:7).

This revelation of His secrets is an indicator of His will to be a personal God. He wants you to know what He is going to do so you become aware of what He is planning. God's plan is not a guarded secret; in fact, it is extraordinarily simple. He wants you to know and understand the fullness of Christ and the message of His shed blood upon the Cross at Calvary.

Points to Ponder

1. Do you believe your wilderness experience is to your benefit? How?

2. "When God pours Himself out to us, He wants to consume us with His very presence. In His presence, there is power and strength." Have you felt His presence lately?

3. Has God revealed His secret for your life to you? Have you been listening for His voice?

Chapter 6

Understanding God's Creation

GOD is using the wilderness experience to restore the mandate for humankind to take dominion and subdue the earth.

> *Then God blessed them, and God said to them, "Be fruitful and multiply; fill the earth and subdue it; have dominion over the fish of the sea, over the birds of the air, and over every living thing that moves on the earth"* (Genesis 1:28).

He is building into your life a divine nature that will enable you to release this supernatural power and give you the strength to overcome the wilderness, cross into the Promised Land, bind the strong man, and receive what is rightfully yours.

> *"The poor and needy seek water, but there is none, their tongues fail for thirst. I, the Lord, will hear them;*

> *I, the God of Israel, will not forsake them. I will open rivers in desolate heights; and fountains in the midst of the valleys; I will make the wilderness a pool of water, and the dry land springs of water. I will plant in the wilderness the cedar and the acacia tree, the myrtle and the oil tree; I will set in the desert the cypress tree and the pine and the box tree together, that they may see and know and consider and understand together, that the hand of the Lord has done this, and the Holy One of Israel has created it* (Isaiah 41:17-20).

The tree imagery mentioned above can be used as symbolic representations of the human personality and varied opportunities God uses to transform you. As you study from this perspective, you will observe that each species has its unique connotation. In verse 19a it states that God "planted" in the wilderness and He "set" in the desert. When God planted something in the wilderness, it references His nature being placed in you at your spiritual birth. This was God's declaration and command that was put inside of you. Then you read in verse 19b that God will "set" in the desert. Desert means "empty heaven." God will fill your emptiness as you live your life. You can say that it is a progression. God will continue to build things in your life.

> *Through wisdom a house is built, and by understanding it is established; by knowledge the rooms are filled with all precious and pleasant riches. A wise man is strong, yes, a man of knowledge increases strength* (Proverbs 24:3-5).

In studying these different trees, we see they have profound meaning. Cedar trees were the prime choices for building ships and particularly for the construction of temples and palaces. King Solomon used this type of wood to build the Temple of Jerusalem. The roof beams as well as the walls were made of cedar wood. Also, the altar in the shrine of the Ark of the Covenant was made of this wood. The high priests, kings, and pharaohs chose cedar wood not only for physical virtues of size and durability, but also for spiritual strength. The physical qualities of the cedar were reflections of the presence of the divine inside of the tree. Cedars were also used for ritual cleansing. Cedar trees symbolized wisdom and strength. You need God's strength to survive in the wilderness. Not only strength, but you also need wisdom on how you can go about your wilderness experience. Cedar also symbolizes the glory of God. You were created to live for the glory of God.

The Holy Spirit protects you from every form of danger that might come to your life.

Acacia trees assume the characteristic of an umbrella-like form. They were strong enough to make furniture, chests, coffins, and bows. It is a hard and durable wood. This wood was used for the construction of the Ark of the Covenant and the Tabernacle. Acacia trees symbolized sensitivity and protection. You need to be sensitive to the Holy Spirit. The Holy Spirit protects you from every form of danger that might come to your life.

Myrtle trees are mentioned as one of the choice plants of the land. It is one of the prophetic pictures of God's promised blessings. Among the Jews it is an emblem of justice. These trees emit perfumes more exquisite than those of a rose. They were used to construct the Feast of Tabernacles. When the Feast of Tabernacles was celebrated by the Jews on the return from Babylon, the people of Jerusalem were ordered to "go forth unto the mount and fetch olive branches and pine branches and myrtle branches, and to make booths." Myrtle trees symbolized unity. Just as God the Holy Spirit and Jesus are united as One, you need to have unity in the Body of Christ.

> *For there are three that bear witness in heaven: the Father, the Word, and the Holy Spirit; and these three are one* (1 John 5:7).

Unity will come only when you work together with others for the Kingdom of God in the Holy Spirit.

Olive trees are one of the safest trees to heat in high temperatures. They can reach a very old age but require a deep, fertile, and well-drained soil. In the Temple of Jerusalem, Solomon used olive wood for the frame of the outer door, the double door of the inner sanctuary, and the two cherubim that stood behind the altar in the Holy of Holies. Olive wood was used as a statement of inner peace. Since this is an inner quality, the olive wood was not outwardly visible because it was covered by gold. Olive trees symbolized perfect peace and the anointing. You need to have perfect peace when you go through your wilderness training. Only Jesus can give you perfect peace that will comfort you no matter what you go through in life. Only through the anointing will you be able to obtain peace in your life.

Cypress trees are large evergreen trees. Since cypress seldom rots, it is used for statues of idols. Just like the cedar wood, cypress trees were used for roof beams of palaces and temples. The wood is very durable and hard. The wood's durability and aromatic scent added to the idol's image. It was also used to build Solomon's Temple. Cypress trees symbolized Heaven's universal calling. God has placed a great calling upon your life. You were called to fulfill the purposes of God in your lifetime.

Pine trees have hard and durable roots. These trees are strongly associated with life force, vitality, death, and resurrection. This wood was used to make crosses for most crucifixions, including that of Jesus Christ. Pine trees symbolize vitality and continuity. In Jesus Christ you have life and because of that you will continue to live. There is no end of life in the Lord.

In Jesus Christ you have life and because of that you will continue to live. There is no end of life in the Lord.

The last type of tree is the box tree. The box is an evergreen, which in our gardens is generally seen only as a dwarf shrub. In the East however, its native country, it attains the size of a forest tree and often forms a very beautiful feature in the landscape. The box tree was peculiarly adapted to the calcareous formations of Mount Lebanon and therefore likely to be brought from coniferous woods for the building of the Temple. Box trees love the sunlight and need good light. As Christians we should love the light and hate darkness. Jesus came as the light of the world. Therefore, we need to let our light shine so brightly before all men that they will know that it is the Lord living inside of us.

These trees are indications of how God is developing you to reflect a life of truth, justice, ritual cleansing, and sustainability. That is why when your identity has been changed, you have been transformed into the image of God. The whole purpose of changing your character is found in Isaiah 41:20, which states, *so that people may see and know, may consider and understand that the hand of the Lord has done this, that the Holy One of Israel created it* (see Isa. 41:20).

God uses tree imagery to represent personalities. As I explained in my first book, *Image of God,* the tree of life in the Garden of Eden represents Jesus. However, this tree can also represent desirable personalities and characteristics such as a wholesome tongue, righteousness, and the stream of God's desire.

Each of these trees is different in their character and nature. It is when the anointing is poured out that God's nature will be formed inside. Those who are chosen will have His Spirit poured upon them. When the anointing is released, He will plant these trees that represent transforming your personalities in the wilderness. God wants to restore His character and nature to all those who believe. When His nature is restored, you can be an instrument for His Kingdom.

Signs and Wonders Released

Once you receive this anointing, it will be the time to experience the supernatural power of God. This is an exciting truth. You already know that God took care of His chosen ones in the wilderness. As you look at the Israelites, you see that He sustained them with water, food, clothing, and security for 40 years.

God wants to fill you with His power so that you can devour the enemy. First John 3:8 states that God sent Jesus so that the enemy's plans would be destroyed: *He who sins is of the devil, for the devil has sinned from the beginning. For this purpose the Son of God was manifested, that He might destroy the works of the devil* (1 John 3:8).

This is why you need to be filled with the anointing. It is so that you can have the same purpose and plan of God. Jesus gave the Church His name to conquer the enemy. However, in order to use it effectively, you need to know Him intimately. Sporadic and weekend experiences with Him will not suffice. You need to make Him the center of your daily life and enter into a lifestyle that honors Him above all others. An example of a shallow and less than personal relationship with Jesus follows in Acts chapter 19.

> *Then some of the itinerant Jewish exorcists took it upon themselves to call the name of the Lord Jesus over those who had evil spirits, saying, "We exorcise you by the Jesus whom Paul preaches." Also there were seven sons of Sceva, a Jewish chief priest, who did so. And the evil spirit answered and said, "Jesus I know, and Paul I know; but who are you?" Then the man in whom the evil spirit was leaped on them, overpowered*

> *them and prevailed against them, so that they fled out of that house naked and wounded. This became known both to all Jews and Greeks dwelling in Ephesus; and fear fell on them all, and the name of the Lord Jesus was magnified* (Acts 19:13-17).

This example demonstrates both the power of Jesus' name and how its misuse leads to failure and humiliation. Like the sons of Sceva, you may know who Jesus is but not acknowledge him as the transformer and personal, physical representation of God upon the earth.

Vision of the Baltimore Dragon

In October 1989, I was praying in the Spirit and experienced an open vision of Baltimore, Maryland. I saw its inner harbor and outside of it a huge, giant dragon had taken the city. As I looked at the head of the creature, a uniformed military official was battling it with an old M1 pistol in his hands. Attached to the weapon was a bayonet, yet even with these weapons, he did not know how to slay the dragon.

I did not quite understand the meaning of the vision and asked God to clarify it. The Lord said, "This soldier represents the churches of Baltimore in the city and suburbs. They do not have enough power to destroy satan's grip over the city." Later in the vision there were a dozen soldiers on top of the dragon and the Lord asked me to move to Baltimore, so I moved there with my wife.

As we approached the city, the dragon disappeared into the sea and my wife and I stopped to eat. Once inside the local restaurant, we noticed it was owned by Asians. However, there were only six people: my wife and I, the owners, and waiters. After ordering, I went to the restroom to wash up and as I exited, a tall waiter holding a syringe of poison confronted me. He grabbed my wife and began trying to stab her with the syringe but I screamed and commanded him to stop. I reached out and placed her behind me so I could fight this demon. During the struggle, I wrestled the syringe from the demon's hands and injected the poison into its body, instantly killing it.

As we approached the city, the dragon disappeared into the sea and my wife and I stopped to eat.

Suddenly, one of the restaurant owners and the remaining waiter were transformed into demons as well. They were hideous and larger than life. I asked the Lord to give me the strength to battle them. All of a sudden Heaven opened and a rod that felt like iron dropped into my hands. In the next moment I began fighting them, ultimately slashing their necks and slaying them. This, of course, was a big spiritual battle and when it was over, I took my wife's hand and led her outside. Upon exiting, we saw a straight highway and green trees on the side of the road. We held hands and began walking toward the roadway and the vision came to a close.

Beyond the Vision

After this vision, the Lord told me to start a church in Baltimore with a call for intercession. I obeyed and planted a church in December 1989 with three families. Since we could not find a facility, we met in a private home and over time our body of believers began to grow. I began visiting other churches, asking to use their facilities. After visiting 27 congregations and being turned down over and over again, we still had no place to call our own. The Lord continued to lead me day by day and I asked the church members to join me in seven days of prayer and fasting.

A month later, God answered our prayers.

After finishing the corporate fast, I received a phone call from a sister in the Lord whom I had met two years ago. She did not know my phone number, nor did I ask how she got it, but she called to provide a word. She asked if I was looking for a church facility and suggested I would find a place in a residential area on top of a local mountain. As I soon learned, she was right. The place did exist and the pastor of the church had recently been planning to go to Korea but God had reassigned him here one month ago.

Even more unique was that this was a Baptist church, yet they were open to the gifts of the Holy Spirit. So based upon the sister's word I called and made an appointment with the pastor. Our meeting was so refreshing. We began in prayer, which was something that none of the other 27 church leaders had done. After a time, I shared why God had brought me to Baltimore and the pastor shared his testimony too. He then listened to my proposal and promised to bring it to the church committee for a decision.

I also found out that another group had previously approached the former pastor with a similar request but their petition had been denied. I asked if the church door could be unlocked in the morning for one week so that we could hold an early morning prayer meeting. Initially four families including mine attended. However, due to snow, the church was closed. Instead of retreating, we stood against the wall and prayed.

A month later God answered our prayers. I received a phone call from the pastor and he said the committee had unanimously agreed to the proposal. We would be meeting in their fellowship hall and both congregations would meet at the same time. Approximately two months later we had a combined church service that hosted over 300 people.

This period of growth was such a blessing. The Lord was leading me by His Spirit and the church was growing and dedicated to intercession. As I drove the beltway around Baltimore, it felt like a triumphant Jericho march. I remained as head pastor in Baltimore for three and a half years, and God asked me to fast and pray for the city because He wanted to bring revival there.

Later I began to recognize that our battle in Baltimore was with various spirits such as Catholicism, fornication, and adultery. These were the spirits that manifested themselves to me in the restaurant. I found out that Baltimore was the first city to permit strip clubs, which opened the door to spirits of fornication and adultery. Yet as we prayed and pressed in, I do believe the atmosphere of the city began to change. We consistently went to the Inner Harbor area to evangelize and our youths were actively involved in street ministry as well.

Unity Is the Key

These days many churches separate themselves from other churches, which simply adds gaps. Since we are not unified, it is difficult to release the power of God. We are Kingdom people belonging to His culture. We need to realize that we are no longer the ethnic race of our youth and that God said there is neither Jew nor Greek, slave or free, men or women, but all are one in Christ (see Gal. 3:28).

Therefore we belong to the family of God. Once this truth is absorbed in our hearts, we can release the power of God in our lives.

Miracles Will Happen

Earlier I described our season of searching for a place to start the Apostles Mission Church in Baltimore. Once the church was established, we held a joyful celebration service. Yet, sadly the next morning I received very heartbreaking news from Korea. My brother-in-law called and told me that my mother had passed away an hour before. I was shocked. I simply did not know how to react because I had not seen my parents in ten years. This decade of separation came from my decision to attend seminary and since they were not believers, I did not tell them of my decision. Only my younger sister knew why I could not go back to Korea. As the only son in the family, I had four older sisters and I paid a great price for His calling. In the Korean culture the son has to take care of the parents, and since I had not been with them for the past ten years, I wanted to catch up with them and spend time with them.

It was around 4 A.M. when I received this news. My wife did not say anything when she heard the news. I put my clothes on and went to the prayer room. I wept and cried. The Lord spoke to me and told me that I should not go to Korea. Instead I was to stay with the church and send my wife. Since I could not go, I grieved but the Lord comforted me, and I continued to pray for my wife during the funeral service in Korea.

The Lord spoke to me and told me that I should not go to Korea.

It should be known that in 1988, I witnessed to my parents and my mother received Jesus Christ. From then on, my mother never missed any morning prayer services. She became a devoted Christian and always prayed for me. My father on the other hand said that he would go to church with my mother but not accept Jesus Christ as his personal Savior until I saw him face to face. It was frustrating because I could not go to the funeral and my wife would be there alone. I asked my father not to pressure or force her to bow down to any idols at the funeral. I also asked my parents' pastor to conduct the funeral. My father still chose to have a subsequent Buddhist-based service.

After the funeral my wife returned home. Five months later my brother-in-law called again. He said that my 84-year-old father was in the intensive care unit with a tumor in his lungs. The growth was very large and the surgeons felt it was too risky to be removed. Strangely, just before my mother had passed, my father had a physical at the hospital and everything was completely normal. He had always gone for annual check-ups and the doctors never noticed any kind of tumors.

During my entire life I never saw my parents fight, and I knew they loved each other very much. After my mother passed away, we asked my father to come to the United States and live with us but he did not want that. My oldest sister who lived nearby chose to care for him instead. The doctors told us that surgery was too risky for him so they knew that the end of his life was very near. I sent my wife ahead of me so I could have an opportunity to ask my associates and the American church pastor to intercede for my father. My wife arrived a day ahead of me and told my father that I would arrive the next day but he simply did not believe it.

**I continued praying,
not knowing how long he would live.**

When I arrived at the hospital, I briefly greeted my sisters and their husbands and then immediately went in to see my father. He could not believe that I was standing in front of him. I asked my father if he remembered the promise he made earlier. He did not say anything but inside I could tell he was ready to accept the Lord. I asked him to pray the sinner's prayer and that day he accepted the Lord Jesus Christ as His

Savior. I continued praying, not knowing how long he would live. At the time I did not know that the head of the Intensive Care Unit (ICU) was a Christian and that her mother was in the same hospital ICU as well.

I did not know what was wrong but I began praying loud enough for all to hear me. The people around me heard my sorrow and brokenness and left my father and I alone for more than 30 minutes. Later I found out that through my intercession, the ICU doctor's mother was completely healed. I stayed with my father for one night and told the doctor that my father should be released because he could not go through with the surgery. The doctor agreed and suggested we go home and just rest. The next day the doctor invited me to breakfast and we sat and talked. She explained the miracle of her mother's recovery and I praised the Lord for what He had done for her.

We then transported my father home and tried our best to care for him. Every time he felt pain he asked me to lay hands on him and pray. As a result he fell asleep without having any pain. After a month of caring for my father, I became exhausted, and my uncle suggested that I should take a few days off to rest. I took my wife and went to her parents' home. On the way I spoke at one church and when we arrived at my in-laws' home, in a vision I saw my father standing up from the coffin. While he was standing, a giant man punched him and he fell back and could not stand up. Immediately I knew that he was ready to go home to the Father in Heaven. I shared this with my wife and told her that we needed to go back immediately.

The next day we met with my father and I could tell he was ready to meet the Lord. With all of us gathered around and holding hands in one accord, my father told me that someone came to take him and told him to change his clothes. We saw that he had total peace and then God welcomed him as he lay there sleeping.

Immediately I knew that he was ready to go home to the Father in Heaven.

On October 18, exactly seven months after my mother had passed away, my father died as well. Later the Lord shared with me the significance of this event. I was so happy that I had spent time with him but I also felt guilty for not seeing them for ten years. The Lord later reassured me that I had given my parents the best gift I could give, which was to lead them into a personal and eternal relationship with God. This was of course a great comfort, and after this word of encouragement, my wife and I returned to the States to continue in our godly calling.

The True Resource

The story of my parents' salvation attests to the greatest gift you can give to people. It is Jesus Christ. You are His true resource, because you know how to reach Him. The people of this earth need to see Christians standing at the top of the mountain being the light so that they will know how to find Him. God made you a valuable person and has shaped your personality like the trees of the Bible to serve His purpose. You need to stand out in this world because you are the light of the world. You must shine brightly so that all men will see God through your life.

Points to Ponder

1. God can fill every emptiness in your life. Can you think of examples when He has done this in the past?

2. Have you experienced an "open vision" like the author did? Do you want to? Why or why not?

3. Have you shared the gift of salvation with your family, friends, and coworkers?

Chapter 7

God Doesn't Give His Praise and Glory to Others

Spiritual Warfare

The Lord shall go forth like a mighty man; He shall stir up His zeal like a man of war. He shall cry out, yes, shout aloud; He shall prevail against His enemies (Isaiah 42:13).

THERE are numerous aspects of spiritual warfare and how it relates to the wilderness that cannot be ignored. As earthly beings who are made of corrupted flesh, you face unique challenges within this asymmetric conflict. God wants you to remain spiritually alert. The Word tells you that you are engaged in a spiritual battle and face an enemy who remains invisible to the naked eye. It is a battle that rages all around you, yet cannot be observed in the natural. Your defense lies within Christ's blood on Calvary and your acceptance that

God provides you the strength to remain on guard so that you may, as Paul states in First Timothy 6:12, "fight the good fight."

> *For we do not wrestle against flesh and blood, but against principalities, against powers, against the rulers of the darkness of this age, against spiritual hosts of wickedness in the heavenly places* (Ephesians 6:12).

Paul's letter to the Ephesians provides a dynamic setting for the battlefield that lies beyond your physical senses. This spiritual battlefield is a war for the mind and is waged by satan who is intent on dominating peoples' lives and challenging God's authority. These two kingdoms have a conflict that is a grand struggle for your life and ultimate freedom. Satan came to dominate, while Jesus came to set the captives free. Isaiah 42:8 states, *I am the Lord, that is My name; and My glory I will not give to another, nor My praise to carved images.*

Since God does not honor or glorify others, there are those who are resistant to Him. The devil has been on the attack ever since his rebellion in the heavens and his campaign of terror which uses deception as the means to devour the unwitting. Even though you cannot see this battle, Christians must be cautious, see its effects, and take refuge in God's Word and warnings.

The Devil and Demons

The devil is a created being that has an organized and functioning kingdom. In that kingdom, there are various areas of responsibility and levels of authority. He has legions of demons to do his bidding and as such they are evil spirits with degrees of leadership and power.

The Devil

Let's examine the different names the Bible uses to describe satan or the devil.

The Prince of the Air

> *In which you once walked according to the course of this world, according to the prince of* ***the power of the air****, the spirit who now works in the sons of disobedience* (Ephesians 2:2).

The title of *prince* speaks of an exalted noble position, and *power* speaks of the realm of that rule, which probably is the area above and around the earth. Since satan is a spirit, he can move through space with considerable speed.

The Prince of This World

> *Now is the judgment of this world; now the ruler of this world will be cast out* (John 12:31).

> *Of judgment, because the ruler of this world is judged* (John 16:11).

Satan is sometimes described as the prince of this world. This means the unregenerate world. It is a world that has fallen from grace and follows him to perdition.

The Prince of Darkness

> *For we do not wrestle against flesh and blood, but against principalities, against powers, against the rulers of the darkness of this age, against spiritual hosts of wickedness in the heavenly places* (Ephesians 6:12).

The darkness theme reveals satan's ultimate nature and his complete disregard for light and holiness. All of his works are black and result in failure.

God of This World

> *Whose minds the god of this age has blinded, who do not believe, lest the light of the gospel of the glory of Christ, who is the image of God, should shine on them* (2 Corinthians 4:4).

Satan is called the god of this age or world and he is the god of pagan people. Many people worship strange idols or objects thinking they are gods, yet ultimately they worship satan who is the supreme pagan deity.

An Angel of Light

> *And no wonder! For Satan himself transforms himself into an angel of light* (2 Corinthians 11:14).

When he is called an angel of light, it is of a deceptive nature. Satan lives to deceive and you can see how deceptive he was in the Garden of Eden. He deceived Adam and Eve into imagining they could be like God, fully enlightened and able to discern good from evil.

Accuser of the Brethren

Then I heard a loud voice saying in heaven; "Now salvation, and strength, and the kingdom of our God, and the power of His Christ have come, for the accuser of our brethren, who accused them before our God day and night, has been cast down" (Revelation 12:10).

One technique the enemy favors is to accuse Christians of always falling short of God's glory. He always looks for ways to accuse the brethren of sin and wants to present a case where they see themselves as guilty.

The Tempter

Now when the tempter came to Him, he said, "If You are the Son of God, command that these stones become bread" (Matthew 4:3).

You know that God does not tempt anyone. The devil is always trying to tempt you to come out of God's protection. Satan's temptations are a plot so that you fall into sin and become overwhelmed by your sin.

Adversary

Be sober, be vigilant; because your adversary the devil walks about like a roaring lion, seeking whom he may devour (1 Peter 5:8).

Scriptures inform you that you have an adversary in your life and it is not others. Instead it is the enemy. Sometimes you may think your adversary is people. However this is what the devil wants you to believe. He is your main adversary. That is why the greatest trick the devil ever conceived was the plan to convince people that he never existed.

An Oppressor

> *God anointed Jesus of Nazareth with the Holy Spirit and with power, who went about doing good and healing all who were oppressed by the devil* (Acts 10:38).

Jesus came to bring about an end to the devil's work. All those who are oppressed by the devil will find freedom in Christ. Jesus came to liberate the people from bondage and to destroy the works of the devil.

Liar

> *You are of your father the devil, and the desires of your father you want to do. He was a murderer from the beginning, and does not stand in the truth, because there is no truth in him. When he speaks a lie, he speaks from his own resources, for he is a liar and the father of it* (John 8:44).

He is always trying to find some ways to accuse you before God. He looks for opportunities when you fall short of God's glory.

Demons

Next, let's look at the characteristics of demons so that as a Christian you can identify them.

Lies

Just like the devil, you must realize that demons are liars, too. Since the devil is the father of lies, demons follow his lead. Their nature is to bring about confusion and deceive people. This is done by spreading lies about you and others.

Power

First, you must recognize that demons have power. However, unlike God, they are not omnipotent. They possess much less power than God and once you are convinced of this truth, you will not be fearful.

> *And if Satan has risen up against himself, and is divided, he cannot stand, but has an end. No one can enter a strong man's house and plunder his goods, unless he first binds the strong man. And then he will plunder his house* (Mark 3:26-27).

> *Then they came to the other side of the sea, to the country of the Gadarenes. And when He had come out of the boat, immediately there met Him out of the tombs a man with an unclean spirit, who had his dwelling among the tombs; and no one could bind him, not even with chains, because he had often been bound with shackles and chains. And the chains had been pulled apart by him, and the shackles broken in pieces; neither could anyone tame him* (Mark 5:1-4).

These verses explain that demons actually do have power to certain degrees. The good news is that their power is limited, while God's power is unlimited. Due to this truth, you do not need to be fearful, because you will always have the victory.

> *Having disarmed principalities and powers, He made a public spectacle of them, triumphing over them in it* (Colossians 2:15).

Doctrine

In these last days demons want to confuse people so they will not know the truth. This is why heresies and unbiblical teachings are spreading across the world.

> *Now the Spirit expressly says that in latter times, some will depart from the faith, giving heed to deceiving spirits and doctrines of demons* (1 Timothy 4:1).

They like to counterfeit everything that is from God. They counterfeit in order to confuse and deceive people. You need to expose these heresies and unbiblical teachings that are influencing many people. Christians need to take a stand against false teachings and carnal philosophies.

Those Who Worship Idols, God Will Chastise

> *They shall be turned back, they shall be greatly ashamed, who trust in carved images, who say to the molded images, You are our gods.... Therefore He has poured on him the fury of His anger and the strength of battle; It has set him on fire all around, yet he did not know; and it burned him, yet he did not take it to heart* (Isaiah 42:17, 25).

God so despises idol worship that his first two commandments to the Israelite nation sharply condemn this behavior. He states that they should not have any other gods before Him and that they should not make any carved images. This of course reflects the nature of the indigenous Palestinian population and their propensity for polytheistic worship of nature (Asherah and Baal). God will bring punishment on those who worship idols, which truly means the worship of satan. He describes the futility of having manmade idols.

> *"Present your case," says the Lord. "Bring forth your strong reasons," says the King of Jacob. "Let them bring forth and show us what will happen; Let them show the former things, what they were, that we may consider them; and know the latter end of them; Or declare to us things to come. Show the things that are to come hereafter, that we may know that you are gods; yes, do good or do evil, that we may be dismayed and see it together. Indeed you are nothing, and your work is nothing. He who chooses you is an abomination.... Indeed they are all worthless, their works are nothing; Their molded images are wind and confusion"* (Isaiah 41:21-24, 29).

God also describes the foolishness of having idols. The reason why they are foolish is because they cannot talk back to people. Here is another verse showing why idols are foolish in God's eyes.

> *Those who make an image, all of them are useless, and their precious things shall not profit; They are their own witnesses; They neither see nor know, that they may be ashamed. Who would form a god or mold an image that*

profits him nothing? Surely all his companions would be ashamed; and the workmen, they are mere men. Let them all be gathered together, let them stand up; Yet they shall fear. They shall be ashamed together. The blacksmith with the tongs works one in the coals. Fashions it with hammers and works it with the strength of his arms.

Even so, he is hungry and his strength fails; He drinks no water and is faint. The craftsman stretches out his rule, he marks one out with chalk; He fashions it with a plane, he marks it out with the compass and makes it like the figure of a man, according to the beauty of a man, that it may remain in the house. He cuts down cedars for himself, and takes the cypress and the oak; He secures it for himself among the trees of the forest. He plants a pine and the rain nourishes it. Then it shall be for a man to burn. For he will take some of it and warm himself; Yes, he kindles it and bakes bread; Indeed he makes a god and worships it; He makes it a carved image and falls down to it. He burns half of it in the fire;

With this half he eats meat; He roasts a roast and is satisfied. He even warms himself and says, "Ah! I am warm. I have seen the fire." And the rest of it he makes into a god, his carved image. He falls down before it and worships it, prays to it and says, deliver me, for you are my god! They do not know nor understand; For He has shut their eyes, so that they cannot see, and their hearts, so that they cannot understand (Isaiah 44:9-18).

God is telling you that idol worship is pointless because it profits no one. The idols cannot see, hear, or speak and men have foolishly believed they have some sort of viable iconic power.

Having a True Character of God

You must have the character and nature of God to be an anointed one of God. Rather than performing miracles, signs, and wonders, building your character is the most important aspect. Character is rarely discussed as the essential quality for a minister. Instead people focus on the exterior of a person's ministry. When they see many miracles, signs, and wonders, the people believe these ministers are true instruments of God. However in the Kingdom of God character determines the validity and integrity of a minister. Due to this truth, God gives His glory to those who know how to handle His glory. God does not need someone who is boastful. Jesus states, you can determine who is a true Christian by observing the fruit of their ministry.

> *Beware of false prophets, who come to you in sheep's clothing, but inwardly they are ravenous wolves. You will know them by their fruits. Do men gather grapes from thorn bushes or figs from thistles? Even so, every good tree bears good fruit, but a bad tree bears bad fruit. A good tree cannot bear bad fruit nor can a bad tree bear good fruit. Every tree that does not bear good fruit is cut down and thrown into the fire. Therefore by their fruits you will know them* (Matthew 7:15-20).

What the Lord is looking for is character. Rather than just judging the outside, God wants you to judge the inside. Our problem in this world of flesh is that we easily marvel and can be influenced by the exterior. Remember it is what's inside, a person's character, that is important.

> *Truly the signs of an apostle were accomplished among you with all perseverance, in signs and wonders and mighty deeds* (2 Corinthians 12:12).

The apostle Paul states that the indications of a true apostle are perseverance, signs and wonders, and mighty deeds. Notice that perseverance is mentioned first. The apostle Paul recognized that being an apostle or any office gift, the foremost sign is found in character. The devil can counterfeit miracles, signs, and wonders but he cannot stand it when true character is manifested because true character overcomes all falsehood. True character always aligns with the truth of God. I believe that the anointing comes to people who have good character above all else. You need to define a person by their fruit and not by their works.

Being humble means allowing or giving God the permission to sit on the throne of your life.

Many people want to start at the top in ministry. They do not realize that ministry starts from the bottom and works its way upward. To be a minister you need to serve from the bottom. This means understanding that you need to get dirty while working at times. To be a minister you need to learn how to serve people first. So for the people who desire to go into ministry, do not be surprised when someone hands you a broom or rag. This is where ministry starts and not at the top. Jesus came to serve first and then miracles followed. Jesus went as far as washing the disciples' feet. Are you willing to wash people's feet?

Being Humble Before the Lord

God gives His glory to those who are humble in spirit. Without being humble, you will abuse your authority. This is why God tests you to see if you will obey His commandments. One thing God loves is obedience. He wants you to be obedient and keep His commands. He does not want you to be obedient so that He can boss you around. Rather, He wants to know if you are for Him and His cause or if you choose to rebel against Him. Being obedient is not a sign of weakness but a sign of strength. It lets you know that you can do nothing without God intervening in your life.

Being humble means allowing or giving God the permission to sit on the throne of your life. It is to let you know that you cannot make it in life if He is not with you. That is why to be obedient means to die. If you examine the word *obedient,* the middle of the word spells out "die." If you die to your plans and agendas, that will enable you to be obedient to the Lord. You will think of serving Him first and foremost.

Another reason for humbling yourself is so pride will not enter your life. I will explain in the next chapter how pride is one of the sins that God does not want you to commit. To be servants of God, you need to be humble.

> *Let this mind be in you which was also in Christ Jesus, who, being in the form of God, did not consider it robbery to be equal with God, but made Himself of no reputation, taking the form of a bondservant, and coming in the likeness of men. And being found in appearance as a man, He humbled Himself and became obedient to the point of death, even the death of the cross. Therefore God also has highly exalted Him and given Him the name which is above every name, that at the name of Jesus every knee should bow, of those in heaven, and of those on earth, and of those under the earth, and that every tongue should confess that Jesus Christ is Lord, to the glory of God the Father* (Philippians 2:5-11).

If this was in Jesus' mind, this should be in your mind as well. When you are humble before the Lord, you will have nothing to lose because you do things His way and not yours. It is better to be exalted by the Lord than to exalt yourself.

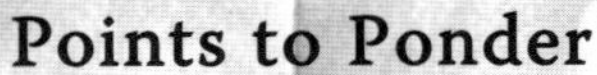

Points to Ponder

1. What or who is satan to you?

2. Do others know you as a person of "good character"?

3. Are you humble enough to allow God to sit on the throne of your life?

Chapter 8

God Will Do New Things

Change Your Mindset

AS fleshly creatures, one of the hardest things for us to do is respond to change. It is especially difficult as we become more and more comfortable with the status quo. Unfortunately, this pattern is particularly true within the Church and is, of course, at odds with God's plan. The foundations of the wilderness plan rely upon our willingness to change and turn away from worldly wisdom. Since God created the world, He knows everything about it. At best, our knowledge is limited. What He wants is to see our understanding replaced with the Word and knowledge of Him. Change is an essential element with God's economy and serves as a basic tenet of life. If we are to prosper, change cannot be avoided.

Forget the Past

Change also signifies a moment when you want the heavens to open so that God's glory can fall. It is a time of celebration and restoration when God is able to restore the Garden of Eden in your heart. This change from suffering to a Garden experience is a means of bringing back the joy you are seeking. Yet, in order for this to take place, the Israelites needed to change their minds so that they could be transformed into a glorious people. The old life, or the wilderness lifestyle, is what needs to be changed. Your periods of complaining and living within negative realms sound to God just like the Israelites who cried out for a return to Egypt. They wanted to go back to their old way of living, even if it meant slavery. However, God is here to restore and He does not want you to spend your time stuck in the past.

> *"Do not remember the former things, nor consider the things of old. Behold, I will do a new thing. Now it shall spring forth; Shall you not know it? I will even make a road in the wilderness"* (Isaiah 43:18-19).

There is no "past" in the wilderness. You should not remember your former life but be excited about your present and future. That means whatever happened in the past remains in the past and is covered by Jesus' death on Calvary. All the things that happened are gone, and you cannot resurrect the past.

> *Brethren, I do not count myself to have apprehended; but one thing I do, forgetting those things which are behind and reaching forward to those*

> *things which are ahead. I press toward the goal for the prize of the upward call of God in Christ Jesus* (Philippians 3:13-14).

Paul was an intelligent man. He was trained professionally and yet he states that those things he learned in the past were of no importance when trying to know God. Having religious knowledge does not make anyone truly knowledgeable about the intimate nature of God. Paul needed an encounter with the Lord to truly know who He was. Without his "Road to Damascus" experience, Paul's understanding would have remained classically intellectual. It is for this reason that God chose to teach Paul through revelation.

> *For I neither received it from man, nor was I taught it, but it came through the revelation of Jesus Christ* (Galatians 1:12).

You need to know the Lord not only from what you have been taught through church, seminary, and Bible school but also through direct revelation. God is still speaking to you today and He wants to reveal Himself, too. Yet in order to experience this revelation, you need to make repairs in your life. You must expect that God will want you to surrender everything that represents your old life so that He can anoint you afresh. I will expand on this later.

Trust God as Provider

It was God who desired to show the Israelites that He was their provider and that He was more than sufficient. As the tribes wandered the Sinai and Negev deserts in temperatures that would kill ordinary people within hours, God provided supernaturally for all their needs. Water, meat, and bread came straight from Heaven. Even their clothes lasted for the 40-year journey.

> *Your garments did not wear out on you, nor did your foot swell these forty years* (Deuteronomy 8:4).

Today, clothing does not last nearly that long, nor do you wear it for 40 years. Every year you buy new things and this shows just how well God provided for His chosen people. What you need to discover is that God is still providing for you as well. His provisions are more than enough and if He tells you that you should not worry about anything then you should trust Him. When God tells you not to worry, He is actually checking your heart.

> *And you shall remember that the Lord your God led you all the way these forty years in the wilderness, to humble you and test you, to know what was in your heart, whether you would keep His commandments or not* (Deuteronomy 8:2).

God wanted the Israelites to be confident that He was their all-sufficient provider. The Israelites needed to discern that when God brought them into the wilderness He assumed complete responsibility for their destiny. They could not make the journey without Him and you need to understand the same principles. Your job is to obey and trust Him.

Deuteronomy 8:3 shows why man should not live by bread alone but needs to live by the Word of God: *So He humbled you, allowed you to hunger, and fed you with manna which you did not know nor did your fathers know, that He might make you know that man shall not live by bread alone; but man lives by every word that proceeds from the mouth of the Lord.*

The wilderness experience was given to teach the ancient and modern children of God how to live by His Word and commandments. We quickly forget the miracles, signs, and wonders that He does in our lives. We need to be constantly reminded of what He did for us. We have all experienced some form of miracle, yet we should not dwell on them. Instead we should focus on the future. This is why sometimes when we worry, it makes us forget God has helped us in the past. Just like the Israelites in the deserts of Egypt, we have a short memory when it comes to God's gracious acts in our lives.

Pray and Study

Here is a chart of what God wants to do in your life. He wants to take you out of Egypt, which is your old, human nature, and bring you into a place where He can transform your mind to that of His.

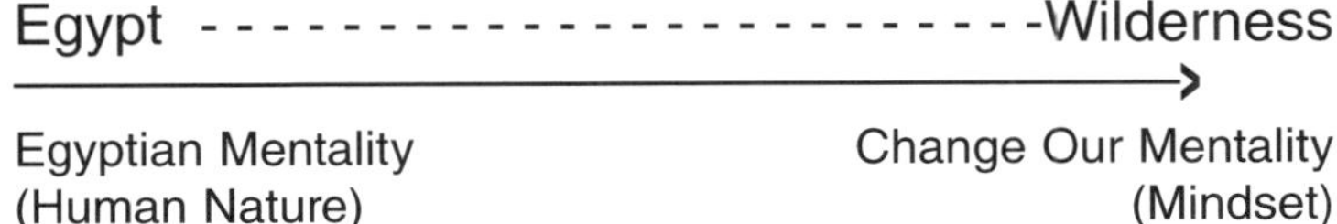

The wilderness exists for you as a means of learning and knowing God's truth. He wants to strip off all wisdom and ways of the world and teach you the ways of His Spirit. This is why sometimes the best way to learn from God is to go through a dry and desolate experience because it causes you to seek God even more. It is where you need to start all over again. Sometimes you need to start from scratch. Just like Paul you may have had “religion or training” but that does not prove that you know Him. You have to allow the Spirit to work in your life. He will be the one who will teach you new knowledge that comes directly from Him and not from the world. In this way, you will become desperate to seek God and hear His voice. As you continue through the wilderness, it will facilitate an adaptation of a lifestyle of prayer and study which identifies the Word as your true source of strength. It was the Spirit that brought Jesus to the wilderness and strengthened Him.

> *Then Jesus, being filled with the Holy Spirit, returned from the Jordan and was led by the Spirit into the wilderness* (Luke 4:1).

The wilderness is a critical time because the experience within it teaches you the value of prayer and the Word as keys to spiritual and physical well-being. It was in the wilderness that Jesus overcame all of satan’s temptations. With this attitude, you will find out that God is the true source of your strength.

Rest in God’s Grace

Another truth about the wilderness is that it is a place to find grace, a place of rest.

> *Thus says the Lord: “The people who survived the sword found grace in the wilderness—Israel, when I went to give him rest”* (Jeremiah 31:2).

Does this verse help you see the wilderness in a different light? Even in dry times, it is a place to find grace from God.

This is why God's grace is more than enough and it is sufficient for you to live by. Are you finding rest in your wilderness experience? The Bible tells you that you will find rest from all your trials, obstacles, and struggles in the wilderness because of His supernatural provision and power.

Another reason why God wants to do new things is because He does not want you to blunder like the Israelites. If you repeat the same errors, then you will never see God do new things. In the Word God notes their cravings and lusts and discusses the five sins they repeated.

> *Now these things became our examples, to the intent that we should not lust after evil things as they also lusted* (1 Corinthians 10:6).

The Five Sins of the Israelites

What are the things that continued to be pitfalls for the Israelites? The answer is within First Corinthians 10:1-13. Let's examine each issue separately to see God's loving warnings.

1. Idol Worship (Idolatry)

> *And do not become idolaters as were some of them* (1 Corinthians 10:7).

The practice of idol worship continued within the Israelite camp, which broke the heart of God because it was an attempt by man to exchange the glory of God with something artificial (man-made).

Professing to be wise, they became fools, and changed the glory of the incorruptible God into an image made like corruptible man (Romans 1:22-23).

They broke the very first commandment of God.

You shall have no other gods before Me (Exodus 20:3).

Since they worshiped other gods, God was not pleased. They did not realize He was jealous of their pagan worship and wanted them to live with the framework of the unique relationship (covenant) as codified by the Torah, Mitzvahs, Commandments, and Law.

Today both Christians and non-Christians still bow down to idols, many of which are now much larger and far more costly than the wooden and stone gods of the ancients. This practice actually means that idol worship has expanded, even though Christianity is the world's most popular religious belief. So then it is fair to ask, "What are the things in your life that have replaced your time with God?" You may spend countless hours doing meaningless activities that fail to promote your relationship with Him.

At the moment Adam and Eve sinned, their relationship with God was cut off.

When the Israelites worshiped other gods, God was not pleased because with their rebellion, they were breaking a relationship with Him. In a very similar manner your human endeavors that consume all of your time serve to breach your living and vibrant relationship with Him. At the moment Adam and Eve sinned, their relationship with God was cut off.

Idolatry is something that you as a Christian need to be aware of because the practice interferes with your relationship with God. It literally traps you within the pitfalls of the images you worship. You may not know that you are spending too much time on other things when you know you need to seek the Lord. This could probably mean that you do not know how to schedule your own life. You may say that you are busy but God gives you enough time to do the things you need to do and seek Him and His Kingdom. What idolatry does is take away your love that was devoted to God. It makes your love for God grow cold.

> *Nevertheless, I have this against you, that you have left your first love* (Revelation 2:4).

> *Jesus answered him, "The first of all the commandments is: 'Hear, O Israel, the Lord our God, the Lord is one. And you shall love the Lord your God with all your heart, with all your soul, with all your mind, and with all your strength.' This is the first commandment. And the second, like it, is this: 'You shall love your neighbor as yourself.' There is no other commandment greater than these"* (Mark 12:29-31).

God wants you to love Him first, before and above all things. That is the first thing Christians need to do. It is to love the Lord first. What idolatry does is to replace or take away your first love. Let's not forget Jesus' words in Revelation and his warning to the Church about turning away from their "first love." The danger of idolatry is that it makes you stop falling in love with the Lord. You need to ask questions to yourself from the perspective of a relationship, and then bluntly ask: "What are the things that are promoting this affair with another?"

> *Examine yourselves as to whether you are in the faith. Test yourselves. Do you not know yourselves, that Jesus Christ is in you?—unless indeed you are disqualified* (2 Corinthians 13:5).

2. Sexual Immorality

> *Nor let us commit sexual immorality* (1 Corinthians 10:8).

We read in the Old Testament how the people of Israel invited foreign people to commit sexual sins with them. These people were the people of Moab.

> *Now Israel remained in Acacia Grove, and the people began to commit harlotry with the women of Moab* (Numbers 25:1).

Due to this act, God commanded Moses to kill all those who committed harlotry. This sight must have been very disturbing to watch as His children abandoned their life of holiness to dine upon pleasures of the flesh.

Yet in the modern era we still live surrounded by temptation. You may question how committed Christians and their leadership could commit sexual immorality or fornication? Frankly, it is because we live in a time when one of God's most precious gifts to humanity has been corrupted. Sex sells. We now exist in an era of visual bombardment with pornographic temptation at our fingertips, in shopping malls, clothing displays, and on television. Physical acts once held precious have been repackaged as a subconscious means of steering people away from God. This industry is one of the wealthiest in the world and it is used by the devil to destroy lives, marriages, and careers.

Sexual immorality is a slippery slope from which very few can self-recover. God wants you to be clean. Sexual sin is the only sin where you can bring unholy things into your body.

> *But he who is joined to the Lord is one spirit with Him. Flee sexual immorality. Every sin that a man does is outside the body, but he who commits sexual immorality sins against his own body. Or do you not know that your body is the temple of the Holy Spirit who is in you, whom you have from God, and you are not your own?* (1 Corinthians 6:17-19).

You need to guard your mind and body through a conscious effort to filter out all impure and profane thoughts. You need to get hold of them before they get hold of you.

> *For though we walk in the flesh, we do not war according to the flesh. For the weapons of our warfare are not carnal but mighty in God for pulling down strongholds, casting down arguments and every high thing that exalts itself against the knowledge of God, bringing every thought into captivity to the obedience of Christ* (2 Corinthians 10:3-5).

Instead, you need to constantly cleanse your mind and bring thoughts to the Cross as you dwell upon things that are holy or pure. You may be asking how you can cleanse your thoughts and not fall into this trap. Philippians 4:8 tells you how.

> *Finally, brethren, whatever things are true, whatever things are noble, whatever things are just, whatever things are pure, whatever things are lovely, whatever things are of good report, if there is any virtue and if there is anything praiseworthy—meditate on these things* (Philippians 4:8).

Satan attacks you in your mind and plays games with you, slowly leading you down mental trails that provide an opportunity for temptation to take root. That is why the battle is always in the mind. Therefore you need a sound counter-strategy that is based upon God. The Bible tells you clearly how you can guard against this temptation. It is not a matter of if satan will attack; it is a matter of when. Ephesians 6:17 states that you need to constantly put the helmet of salvation on your head, to protect you from any evil ideas.

Satan is especially talented at tempting and twisting God's Word for his advantage. The devil's ideas distort your thinking and lead you to see things through a lens of lust. This is why you must protect your mind and "flee from evil."

Abstain from every form of evil (1 Thessalonians 5:22).

3. Tempting God

Nor let us tempt Christ (1 Corinthians 10:9).

The Israelites tempted the Lord when they were stuck with no water. They wondered if God was truly among them. They wanted to see proof of His presence when they complained to Moses about their lack of water.

> *Therefore the people contended with Moses, and said, "Give us water, that we may drink." So Moses said to them, "Why do you contend with me? Why do you tempt the Lord?" So he called the name of the place Massah and Meribah, because of the contention of the children of Israel, and because they tempted the Lord, saying, "Is the Lord among us or not?"* (Exodus 17:2,7).

The way the Israelites tempted God was to challenge His presence for something that was tangible, something that they could define with their senses. In addition, their dispute was a challenge to His authority and power. They quickly forgot the Red Sea experience and they were once again demanding more proof of His existence, presence, and intention.

This can also be a mistake we make with God. We may be tempting God for something we need in life. One way that we tempt God is asking for something and promising that if we get it, we will devote more time to doing God's work. Just as the ancients wanted visual proof, we also want assurances. In many ways our postmodern era of enhanced technology and materialism serves to block faith in what God can do. As Westerners we have been taught to believe in the tangible—"if you cannot see or feel something, it must not be real."

Another way we tempt God is by contending with the leaders over us. As we examine Exodus 17:2, it states that people were challenging Moses about water. Their demands for water were actually a means of tempting God, because they knew Moses had access to Him. If they did not get the water, they wanted to go back to Egypt. As we examine our lives, the way we may tempt God is by contending with our spiritual leadership. When we do not like what that leader is doing or have some sort of disagreement, we may start to confront the leader or threaten with materialistic things.

Another way we tempt God is by contending with the leaders over us.

For example, if there is a wealthy person in the church, it seems like that wealthy person has power to do whatever they want because of their financial contributions. If they do not like what is going on and do not get their way, they may threaten to leave the congregation. When they leave the church, they say that the church will be in trouble financially. This is one way where people may be tempting God.

Another way is when God wants to take the church to their destiny but tradition will not allow it. Tradition will stir up the people to contend against any change. People start to get offended and leave because the church is doing new things. This is why the leader of the church cannot always please everybody.

4. Complaining and Murmuring Against God

The Israelites murmuring against God and Moses was a consistent feature of their post-Egyptian experience. Their complaining was provoking the Lord for it appears that they had forgotten what the Lord did for them in spite of their salvation from Egypt. They were still ungrateful to the Lord.

> *Then the whole congregation of the children of Israel complained against Moses and Aaron in the wilderness* (Exodus 16:2).

When you start to complain, you tend to bring other people into your cause. Complaining and murmuring will always cause division in the Church.

> *...nor complain* (1 Corinthians 10:10).

It will bring disunity and factions. It usually begins when people start gossiping against one another. Complaining also shows that you are never satisfied with what you have. The Israelites were never satisfied with what the Lord provided for them either. They kept on desiring to go back to Egypt because they were concerned about their stomach more than their allegiance to God. When you start to complain or murmur, it shows that you are not content with what you have. Contentment does not come through what you can obtain. It comes from God.

> *Now godliness with contentment is great gain. For we brought nothing into this world and it is certain we can carry nothing out* (1 Timothy 6:6-7).

Here you can see that contentment comes from being a godly person. The true source of contentment lies in becoming a man or woman of God. It is not how much you can store up on earth. As the Word states, you cannot take anything with you upon death. Rather, contentment is from being a person filled with God's Spirit. Contentment states that godliness is great gain. What can a person gain from practicing godliness? They gain something that the enemy has no answers to. It is joy in the Holy Spirit.

> *For the kingdom of God is not eating and drinking, but righteousness and peace and joy in the Holy Spirit.* (Romans 14:17).

Jesus states that no one will be able to take away your joy, and that includes the devil.

> *Therefore you now have sorrow; but I will see you again and your heart will rejoice, and your joy no one will take from you. Until now you have asked nothing in My name. Ask, and you will receive, that your joy may be full* (John 16:22,24).

Satan has no power to take joy from you. God wants to restore your joy.

5. Pride

Now we come to the last sin that Paul tells us the Israelites committed against God.

> *Therefore let him who thinks he stands take heed lest he fall* (1 Corinthians 10:12).

During the wilderness experience, God wanted to see if the Israelites were going to walk in His ways. He wanted to test their faithfulness and allegiance. When things get comfortable for you, you can think that everything was gained through your own efforts, strength, and gifts.

Beware that you do not forget the Lord your God by not keeping His commandments, His judgments and His statutes which I command you today, lest—when you have eaten and are full, and have built beautiful houses and dwell in them; and when your herds and your flocks multiply and your silver and your gold are multiplied and all that you have is multiplied; when your heart is lifted up and you forget the Lord your God who brought you out of the land of Egypt, from the house of bondage (Deuteronomy 8:11-14).

In these verses above, God warns the Israelites that even when times become prosperous, it is not the most important thing. Instead, they were to value keeping His commandments and statutes. This same principle applies to you today. When you become successful, you need to make sure that you do not forget about the commands and statutes of God. It is very simple and easy to get caught up with the things of the world.

Another thing about pride is that it will cause rebellion. The Israelites were always thinking that it was their righteousness that defeated their enemies. However, the Bible tells us that God defeated all of Israel's enemies because they were wicked.

Do not think in your heart, after the Lord your God has cast them out before you, saying, 'Because of my righteousness the Lord has brought me in to possess this land'; but it is because of the wickedness of these nations that the Lord is driving them out from before you.

It is not because of your righteousness or the uprightness of your heart that you go in to possess their land, but because of the wickedness of these nations that the Lord your God drives them out from before you, and that He may fulfill the word which the Lord swore to your fathers, to Abraham, Isaac, and Jacob. Therefore understand that the Lord your God is not giving you this good land to possess because of your righteousness, for you are a stiff-necked people.

Remember! Do not forget how you provoked the Lord your God to wrath in the wilderness. From the day that you departed from the land of Egypt until you came to this place, you have been rebellious against the Lord (Deuteronomy 9:4-7).

You need to be very careful of not exalting yourself. Each time the Israelites were prideful, they always rebelled against God. They always thought that since God was on their side, they were invincible and powerful but it was because other nations were wicked in the eyes of God. You may take being a Christian for granted at times. Yet the best antidote for pride is to humble yourself and be dependent upon God. People want to be independent and live the way they want and not according to God's standards. This is why many people love the world, and when they do they become enemies of God.

Do not love the world or the things in the world. If anyone loves the world, the love of the Father is not in him (1 John 2:15).

> *Adulterers and adulteresses! Do you not know that friendship with the world is enmity with God? Whoever therefore wants to be a friend of the world makes himself an enemy of God* (James 4:4-5).

These are valuable lessons that you need to learn from the Israelites. God does not want you to commit the same sins they committed. Their actions caused them to wander through the wilderness for 40 years before crossing into the Promised Land. God's desire is that you go through your wilderness experience knowing the true purpose of the journey. Paul warns Christians that warnings are for our examples.

> *Now all these things happened to them as examples, and they were written for our admonition, upon whom the ends of the ages have come* (1 Corinthians 10:11).

The tone is very serious and we need to understand that these warnings are recorded so we do not commit similar follies. These were the ways that the Israelites were living in the flesh and God wanted to strip this off of them in the wilderness.

The wilderness has been provided to change us and not the situation we are in. God is more interested in changing our lives—since situations will always exist. In the wilderness everything that does not resemble God must be stripped off. We must make every effort to live by God's standards and make it a high priority in our lives because it will help protect us from the enemy. The enemy will not rest until he sees God's people fall, so as Christians we need to take the Word of God as our standard for living in all we do.

Points to Ponder

1. Have you surrendered *everything* that represents your old life so that God can anoint you afresh?

2. *"Therefore understand that the Lord your God is not giving you this good land to possess because of your righteousness, for you are a stiff-necked people."* Rewrite this Scripture in your mind to apply to your humbleness before a mighty God.

3. Will you search for purpose and meaning while in the wilderness, or will you complain and wander aimlessly?

Chapter 9

Power to Obtain Wealth

And you shall remember the Lord your God, for it is He who gives you power to get wealth, that He may establish His covenant which He swore to your fathers, as it is this day... (Deuteronomy 8:18).

HOW does the wilderness experience fit in with you having the power to become wealthy? Some people might say that the purpose of the wilderness is to fulfill your spiritual needs rather than financial or physical needs. This is true but God also has a plan for His people to obtain greater measures of wealth. One of the lies taught about resources is that holy people should be poor. This concept of poverty and piety was established in the Dark Ages by monastic orders of Catholic monks who were reacting to the audacious wealth, greed, and corruption of the Roman Church. In those circumstances it may have seemed right, but the truth is poverty is a curse that has kept many talented and anointed people from fulfilling their God-given destiny. They see how hard it is to simply survive and decide that living in poverty is no way to exist. The idea that poverty is a sign of humility and devotion to the Lord is simply false. If it were true, the wretched poor within the "10-40 Window" would have no need of evangelization.

> *For the love of money is a root of all kinds of evil, for which some have strayed from the faith in their greediness, and pierced themselves through with many sorrows* (1 Timothy 6:10).

God is the one paying you, not your secular boss.

The truth the apostle Paul is trying to tell us is that the love of money is the root of all kinds of evil. As the previous chapter noted, when you place something else such as wealth ahead of the Lord, then you are in sin. So having money is not evil but loving money more than God is evil. In addition this idea begins to lead you down an additional logical road. If God is a rich God, why would He want His children to be poor? If God has everything, why would He want His children or servants to have nothing? Since when has it been a parent's dream or goal to see their children in poverty? As a matter of fact, the majority of parents strive to make things better for their children, not worse! So then why would God want you to be poor? Is it so that you cannot do anything but starve or worry? That is why you need to know the truth about money or wealth.

God has given you the power to obtain wealth for one reason—so that His Kingdom will be expanded and He will be glorified. Yet many Christians still do not recognize this fact. They have the mentality that since they work hard, they may use money as they wish. The big mistake in this thinking is that they fail to recognize who is the Boss. God is the one paying you, not your secular boss. God pays all of your bills and when He tests you, He does so through money since this is where your true heart and treasure will be.

> *Do not lay up for yourselves treasures on earth, where moth and rust destroy and where thieves break in and steal; but lay up for yourselves treasures in heaven, where neither moth nor rust destroys and where thieves do not break in and steal. For where your treasure is, there your heart will be also* (Matthew 6:19-21).

When you give to the Lord, especially with tithes and offerings, He is always looking at the depth of the sacrifice. We see this in Mark 12:41-44:

> *Now Jesus sat opposite the treasury and saw how the people put money into the treasury. And many who were rich put in much. Then one poor widow came and threw in two mites, which make a quadrans. So He called His disciples to Himself and said to them, "Assuredly, I say to you that this poor widow has put in more than all those who have given to the treasury; for they all put in out of their abundance, but she out of her poverty put in all that she had, her whole livelihood."*

Jesus was looking especially at what proportion people would give to God. This is why God always tests you with money.

> *Will a man rob God? Yet you have robbed Me! But you say, 'In what way have we robbed You?' In tithes and offerings. You are cursed with a curse, for you have robbed Me. Even this whole nation. Bring all the tithes into the storehouse, that there may be food in My house, and try Me now in this, says the Lord of hosts. If I will not open for you the windows of heaven and pour out for you such blessing, that there will not be room enough to receive it. And I will rebuke the devourer for your sakes so that he will not destroy the fruit of your ground, nor shall the vine fail to bear fruit for you in the field, says the Lord of hosts; And all nations will call you blessed. For you will be a delightful land, says the Lord of hosts* (Malachi 3:8-12).

These verses tell you that tithes will open up the heavens for you so that blessings will come. If you want these blessings to come, you also need to know one other aspect. What will actually cause the blessings to come? You need to think about the 90% that is left after you tithed. What do you do with the 90% that is left? Many spend it on their own pleasures and desires.

However, if you sow into the Kingdom of God, you will reap a harvest. God wants you to invest His money into His Kingdom. You can either be stingy and selfish with your money or have a giving attitude and spirit. For Matthew 6:24 states, *No one can serve two masters; for either he will hate the one and love the other, or else he will be loyal to the one and despise the other. You cannot serve God and mammon.*

If you love money and place it ahead of God's Kingdom, you will ultimately be separated because you have made a choice to serve wealth rather than the Creator who is the provider of all wealth. You should not follow money but money should follow you. This is why you need to understand the true meaning of having these resources. It is not for your own pleasure but for the Kingdom of God. You need to invest your money for this cause. The more you invest in God's Kingdom, the more will come to you.

How to Have the Power to Get Wealth

Now that you understand its true meaning, how do you obtain the power to get wealth? First of all, wealth does not come automatically. God wants you to work for it. The secret lies in having the anointing of God. It is not a step-by-step formula to follow, which probably most people reading this book wish it were. It is through the anointing of God that you have the power to get wealth. That is why without the anointing of God, we cannot do anything. The anointing of God teaches you all things. First John 2:20,27 reads, *But you have an anointing from the Holy One, and you know all things. But the anointing which you have received from Him abides in you, and you do not need that anyone teach you; but as the same anointing teaches you concerning all things, and is true, and is not a lie, and just as it has taught you, you will abide in Him.*

God's Word says that since you have the anointing, you don't need to have someone teach you but rather you are to exercise your own creativity. It is through the anointing that He gave you a creative mind. The anointing gives you the creativity and shows you opportunities to expand the Kingdom. The key is that God has given everyone creativity. Since the Creator is inside of you, He wants you to use the anointing to create opportunities for wealth.

We need to learn how to use the things God has given us to achieve prosperity.

The problem is not getting wealth, but it lies in the fact that we are not being creative in getting wealth or money. God is waiting for us to use our creativity in bringing the wealth of the sinners to the righteous. We need to learn how to use the things God has given us to achieve prosperity.

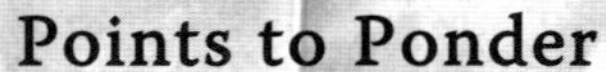

Points to Ponder

1. Do you believe that "holy people should be poor"?

2. How can you use your resources to further His Kingdom on earth?

3. Is there anybody or anything that comes before God in your life?

Chapter 10

Prepare the Heart of the Father

Formation of a Father's Heart

THE wilderness was not created so that it could only serve a single function. Instead it was designed to produce people who in addition to receiving an anointing could be developed with a Father's heart. As a result, those who have been formed within the fires of this crucible have been developed in a unique way. Let's review examples from the Old and New Testaments.

Father in the Faith

The Old Testament portrays Elijah living a solitary life in the wilderness where he received a special revelation from God. The Lord told him to go to the top of a mountain and wait for Him there. The Lord came in a "still small voice," which led Elijah to anoint two kings and a prophet (see 1 Kings 19:11-18). As the story unfolds, Elisha follows Elijah because the mantle was thrown upon him. What you observe is the stirring of a Father's heart in Elijah, whose new task is to train and prepare Elisha for service as a future prophet. In following the Lord's commands, Elijah became a father figure to Elisha.

A father in the faith will attract followers.

You read that Elisha went wherever Elijah went. He would never leave the presence of Elijah and was chasing after his spiritual father to learn from him. A true father in the faith has something to impart to his children. Elisha knew that Elijah had things in his life that could be imparted. A father in the faith will attract followers, whether it be one or ten or hundreds. When Elijah went to Heaven, Elisha continued in Elijah's footsteps and ultimately surpassed him. In this case the wilderness was used as a time and place for God to train His people.

Fathers in the Faith

John the Baptist came in the spirit and power of Elijah, following the same pattern of wilderness solitude. It was through the wilderness experience that he grew in the spirit and power of Elijah.

So the child [**John the Baptist**] *grew and became strong in spirit, and was in the deserts till the day of his manifestation to Israel"* (Luke 1:80).

God's Word came to John the Baptist in the wilderness just like it came to Elijah in the wilderness.

> *...while Annas and Caiaphas were high priests, the word of God came to John the son of Zacharias in the wilderness* (Luke 3:2).

It was in the wilderness that John received the revelation of the impending Kingdom of God and a command to prepare the way. His method for preparing the way was through preaching a baptism of repentance for the remission of sins, because the Kingdom of God was at hand.

> *In those days John the Baptist came preaching in the wilderness of Judea, and saying, "Repent, for the kingdom of heaven is at hand!"* (Matthew 3:1-2)

The father's heart that was being formed in John was one that led him to turn the fathers' hearts back to their children and the children's hearts back to their fathers (see Mal. 4:6). He was sent as a mediator and arbiter of reconciliation between fathers and sons. God formed John's fatherly heart in the desert. A father figure is needed to lead his people and provide a role model as a leader of the family.

A father figure is needed to lead His people and provide a role model as a leader of the family.

Another father figure in the faith is the apostle Paul. He was a father to many, but two early Church leaders stand out.

The first person is Titus. Titus was a young leader in the midst of being prepared for greater ministry responsibilities. Paul taught and trained Titus in everything he knew in ministry. He was so confident in Titus's preparation that he sent him as his proxy to establish churches.

> *For this reason I left you in Crete, that you should set in order the things that are lacking, and appoint elders in every city as I commanded you* (Titus 1:5).

A true father in the faith knows when to release his children to do the work of God. Paul taught Titus how to appoint leaders in churches, since he could see a time when Titus would have to do this on his own accord.

The second person of interest is Timothy. Paul charged him to teach what he had learned to other people. In addition he encouraged Timothy to persevere like a soldier because there would be many obstacles and battles in his ministry. In Second Timothy 2:2-3, Paul writes to guide him and fortify him as he faces growing opposition: *And the things that you have heard from me among many witnesses, commit these to faithful men who will be able to teach others also. You therefore must endure hardship as a good soldier of Jesus Christ.*

While Timothy was learning from Paul, he was also teaching others. Paul saw he was capable of teaching the Word of God to others. Since Paul knew what would occur in ministry, he also warned Timothy in advance of the dangers ahead.

The apostle Paul calls these two men his sons in the faith. Fathers in the faith know how to train their children. They spend most of their time training and being with their children. Fathers want their children to be firmly established and ready to go achieve things greater than they did. While the children are being trained, they are also training others. It becomes a chain reaction.

Fathers want their children to be firmly established and ready to go achieve things greater than they did.

When fathers train their children, they pass their inheritance and, in time, generation upon generation of spiritual fathers are discovered, groomed, and released. Paul would not have been able to impart to these spiritual sons if he himself did not experience the same things in his lifetime. Fathers learn many things in the wilderness so that they can teach their children not to repeat the same mistakes. Fathers are the ones who have the experience and know how to overcome.

Points to Ponder

1. How would you describe your relationship with your earthly father?

2. Do you judge your heavenly Father by the way your earthly father treated you?

3. Have you forgiven your earthly father for anything that you may still hold against him? Why or why not?

Chapter 11

The Promised Land

OUR goal or destination is to reach the Promised Land. God wants to bring us to a place where we can daily experience living in the Spirit of God. This is what God intended to do for the Israelites. He wanted to give them a new life with a new identity. He wanted them to dwell in a land that was fruitful and plentiful.

Let's look at Deuteronomy 8:7-9: *For the Lord your God is bringing you into a good land, a land of brooks of water, of fountains and springs, that flow out of valleys and hills; a land of wheat and barley, of vines and fig trees and pomegranates, a land of olive oil and honey; a land in which you will eat bread without scarcity, in which you will lack nothing; a land whose stones are iron and out of whose hills you can dig copper.*

Before you can go and possess the Promised Land, you need to die on the Cross and receive the anointing of God at the Jordan River. The Jordan River symbolizes death. Unless you are crucified with Christ and die to this world, you cannot go any further because you would not have the anointing.

The anointing is crucial because without it, you will not be able to defeat the enemies living in your land.

GIANTS IN THE LAND

The Promised Land was a place God promised to the Israelites. That is why when they were near the land God told Moses to send out spies to investigate the land.

> *And the Lord spoke to Moses, saying, "Send men to spy out the land of Canaan, which I am giving to the children of Israel; from each tribe of their fathers you shall send a man, every one a leader among them"* (Numbers 13:1-2).

When Israel first approached the land of Canaan, they sent out a group of 12 spies, one from each tribe of Israel, to gather intelligence and information on the Canaanites. The spies went all the way through the land of Canaan and returned in fear from what they saw. All but two, Joshua and Caleb, brought horrifying news of the people living in the land. They saw that there were giants living in the land and these giants were the sons of Anak. We read about this in Numbers 13:33:

> *There we saw the giants (the descendants of Anak came from the giants); and we were like grasshoppers in our own sight, and so we were in their sight.*

This report brought fear to the Israelites and they did not want to enter the land. Even though the Israelites had seen many supernatural signs and wonders, they still were not convinced that God was omnipotent and that no force in Heaven or on earth could defeat Him or those who were with Him.

The sons of Anak were giants that were produced by the Rephaim giants in the land of Canaan. They were the strongest, fastest, and fiercest of their day. They were greatly feared by all other inhabitants who were other giants living in that land (I will expand on the Rephaim giants later). They were belligerent people who loved war and regarded it as a normal way of life. These people were so wild and warlike that when they had no enemies to fight, they fought each other.

These people were so wild and warlike that when they had no enemies to fight, they fought each other.

When the Israelites wanted to go back to Egypt, God was so angry with them that He wanted to destroy them right then. Moses however interceded and God had a pardoning heart. We read about this in Numbers 14:11-12, 19-20: *Then the Lord said to Moses: "How long will these people reject Me? And how long will they not believe Me, with all the signs which I have performed among them? I will strike them with the pestilence and disinherit them, and I will make of you a nation greater and mightier than they." "Pardon the iniquity of this people, I pray, according to the greatness of Your mercy, just as You have forgiven this people, from Egypt even until now." Then the Lord said: "I have pardoned, according to your word."*

After God's pardon He barred their exit from the wilderness for the next 40 years. It was His plan to use this time to purify the nation, and all who showed no faith in Him would never cross the river Jordan. That is why only two survivors, Joshua and Caleb, crossed over, because they had faith that God would lead them to victory.

> *Then Caleb quieted the people before Moses, and said, "Let us go up at once and take possession, for we are well able to overcome it"* (Numbers 13:30).

They believed that their faith in the Lord was enough to defeat the giants regardless of their great size and strength. They knew that it was not by might or by power but through God's Spirit that they would conquer them. So during these 40 years of spiritual training in the wilderness, a new generation of Israelites grew up in an environment that solely relied on God for survival. As a result they were now ready to take on these giants and defeat them with the help of the Lord.

You need to understand that the Lord fights your battles. All you need to do is to trust and have faith in Him for deliverance.

The reason why you need the anointing is because there are many giants living in the Promised Land. There were particularly seven tribes of giants possessing the land.

> *And Joshua said, "By this you shall know that the living God is among you, and that He will without fail drive out from before you the Canaanites and the Hittites and the Hivites and the Perizzites and the Girgashites and the Amorites and the Jebusites* (Joshua 3:10).

The Rephaim Giants

You need to understand the significance of these tribes. These tribes were the next generation of giants of Nephilim called the Rephaim. Nephilim were the gigantic offspring that resulted from the union of the fallen sons of God and the daughters of men that were half-divine, half-human demigods.

> *Now it came to pass, when men began to multiply on the face of the earth, and daughters were born to them, that the sons of God saw the daughters of men, that they were beautiful; and they took wives for themselves of all whom they chose. And the Lord said, "My Spirit shall not strive with man forever, for he is indeed flesh; yet his days shall be one hundred and twenty years." There were giants on the earth in those days, and also afterward, when the sons of God came in to the daughters of men and they bore children to them. Those were the mighty men who were of old, men of renown* (Genesis 6:1-4).

These sons of God were actually angels that came down from Heaven. These verses will tell you that the sons of God were actually angels who went before God's presence.

> *Now there was a day when the sons of God came to present themselves before the Lord, and Satan also came among them* (Job 1:6).

> *Again there was a day when the sons of God came to present themselves before the Lord, and Satan came*

> *also among them to present himself before the Lord* (Job 2:1).

> *To what were its foundations fastened? Or who laid its cornerstone, when the morning stars sang together, and all the sons of God shouted for joy?* (Job 38:6-7).

These Rephaim were of Amorite descent. The Rephaim, mighty warriors and chariot riders, were described as divine beings and human beings, and they functioned like the Amorite god of Baal. The Amorites worshiped Baal and they believed that Baal was also gigantic in stature.

The Seven Deadly Tribes of the Canaanites

These seven tribes also represented certain sins or spirits in life that must be utterly destroyed. Seven in the Bible means completion. So these seven deadly sins or spirits must be completely destroyed in our lives. We can find these sins listed in the Book of Proverbs. There are six things that the Lord hates, seven that are actually abominable to Him.

> *These six things the Lord hates, yes, seven are an abomination to Him: A proud look, a lying tongue, hands that shed innocent blood, a heart that devises wicked plans, feet that are swift in running to evil, a false witness who speaks lies, and one who sows discord among brethren* (Proverbs 6:16-19).

No wonder the Lord commanded the Israelites to destroy these giants. These giants were such an abomination that He did not want any survivors left. The very reason could be that He did not want any more of these giants to reproduce. When God wants you to repent of your sins, He does not want you to go back to them again. They need to be totally gone in your life.

The World System

> *Here is the mind which has wisdom: The seven heads are seven mountains on which the woman sits. These will make war with the Lamb, and the Lamb will overcome them, for He is Lord of lords and King of kings, and those who are with Him are called, chosen, and faithful. For God has put it into their hearts to fulfill His purpose, to be of one mind, and to give their kingdom to the beast, until the words of God are fulfilled* (Revelation 17:9,14,17).

These verses describe the mystery of Babylon and what will happen. You need to understand that the seven mountains mentioned here symbolize the system of Babylon. The system of Babylon is actually the world system. The world system is contrary to the purpose of God. God will destroy the world system and every enemy that arises against His Kingdom. This is the enemy that you need to annihilate. You have been taught and brought up by this world system and now God wants to bring you up in His Kingdom statutes. God wants His rule and reign to be upon all people.

> *But the court shall be seated, and they shall take away his dominion, to consume and destroy it forever. Then the kingdom and dominion, and the greatness of the kingdoms under the whole heaven, shall be given to the people, the*

> *saints of the Most High. His kingdom is an everlasting kingdom, and all dominions shall serve and obey Him* (Daniel 7:26-27).

In the Book of Daniel it talks about four kingdoms that will arise to power. However, these four kingdoms will not last because there will arise another kingdom that is everlasting. God's Kingdom will totally destroy all His enemies. This is why all sins and everything that is against the sovereignty of God must be destroyed in your life. It is so that all men will serve and obey Him.

Now let's go back to the giants that were living in the Promised Land. These giants were dwelling in the land that the Lord had given to the Israelites. You need to understand how big these giants were. An example of how big they were is a description of the bed of the king of Og.

> *For only Og king of Bashan remained of the remnant of the giants. Indeed his bedstead was an iron bedstead. (Is it not in Rabbah of the people of Ammon?) Nine cubits is its length and four cubits is its width, according to the standard cubit* (Deuteronomy 3:11).

Let's calculate this. One cubit is equal to 17.5 inches. Nine cubits times 17.5 cubits is equal to 157.5. Then you divide it by 12 and get 13 feet. Four cubits times 17.5 is equal to 70. You divide that by 12 and get 5.8 feet. He was 13 feet by 5.8 feet!

The Lord gave specific instructions to the Israelites on how to deal with these giants. He told them to utterly destroy all of them.

> *Speak to the children of Israel, and say to them: "When you have crossed the Jordan into the land of Canaan, then*

> *you shall drive out all the inhabitants of the land from before you, destroy all their engraved stones, destroy all their molded images, and demolish all their high places* (Numbers 33:51-52).

> *When the Lord your God brings you into the land which you go to possess and has cast out many nations before you, the Hittites and the Girgashites and the Amorites and the Canaanites and the Perizzites and the Hivites and the Jebusites, seven nations greater and mightier than you, and when the Lord your God delivers them over to you, you shall conquer them and utterly destroy them. You shall make no covenant with them nor show mercy to them* (Deuteronomy 7:1-2).

These giants caused all sorts of problems since the Israelites were afraid of them due to their size and strength. The Israelites did not really believe that they could destroy all these giants even when the Lord told them that He would give them into their hands. That was why the Lord was allowing them to go through the wilderness so that they could get rid of their flesh mindset and be transformed by the power of God. However, God had to wait until the generation that came out of Egypt had died because they showed a lack of belief and trust in the Lord and continued to do evil before the eyes of God.

> *So the Lord's anger was aroused against Israel, and He made them wander in the wilderness forty years, until all the generation that had done evil in the sight of the Lord was gone* (Numbers 32:13).

God was looking for a generation that would not think twice about what He said. He was looking for a generation that would be obedient and not afraid of the odds against them. God was looking for people who were fearless, who knew no fear against the enemy or the odds they faced. Joshua and Caleb knew that God was able and that He would help them regardless of how outnumbered they were. That is why they were able to go possess the Promised Land. As the people feared how big and strong the inhabitants were, Joshua and Caleb still believed in the Lord. They believed that they were able to possess the land. They had no hesitation and knew they were destined to occupy it.

They knew they were destined to occupy it.

When God tells you to do something, you should not hesitate, but be obedient because hesitation is a sign of unbelief. When you are hesitating, you are beginning to question everything instead of trusting in God.

God Deals With the Heart

What God was dealing with the Israelites about was their heart. He wanted to know what was really inside of them. You need to realize that the biggest challenge you have is the inside of your heart. God is giving us the same instructions about sin in our lives. We have to utterly destroy all the things in our heart that make us compromise. God does not want us to compromise with any sin that we may have committed.

He actually does not want us to show any mercy to our sin. How do we show mercy to sin? By not confessing, repenting of, and renouncing sin.

We need to be cleansed daily. If we continue to compromise with our sins, it will eventually ruin and destroy our lives. If we continue to compromise, our conscience will condemn us. Due to this we may not be able to experience the fullness of God in our lives. That is why we need to experience the power of God and receive the anointing.

Our heart has to be cleansed so that we can cast out all sin. Isaiah 52:1-2 encourages us to *Awake, awake! Put on your strength, O Zion; Put on your beautiful garments, O Jerusalem, the holy city! For the uncircumcised and the unclean shall no longer come to you. Shake yourself from the dust, arise; sit down, O Jerusalem! Loose yourself from the bonds of your neck, O captive daughter of Zion!*

Only God's power can deliver the person out of their bondage.

We need to understand that the Canaanites could not be defeated with natural power and strength. Yet the Israelites could only see things from this perspective. They saw how weak they were against the Canaanites. We cannot destroy sins in our lives with natural power. That is why psychology, other areas of human rationale, fortunetellers, and psychics cannot destroy your sins. As Zechariah 4:6 states, *"Not by might nor by power, but by My Spirit," says the Lord of hosts.*

Only God's power can deliver the person out of their bondage. Due to seeking help from ungodly sources, people fail many times and fall short of God's glory. We cannot continue trying to solve our problems without God's anointing.

God not only told the Israelites to utterly destroy the giants but also to take their riches and wealth. God wants to give us the benefits of what the Promised Land offers, and He blesses us once we are obedient to His will.

Points to Ponder

1. Have you ever seen a situation different from what others saw? Were you bold enough to speak out?

2. The world system is the opposite of God's Kingdom system. Think of ways you can help bring His Kingdom come on earth as it is in Heaven.

3. Only the blood of Jesus has the power to eliminate sin from our lives. Think of other ways people try to free themselves from sin—to no avail.

Chapter 12

The Making of an Anointed One

The Anointing

THE pinnacle of your wilderness experience is when you receive the anointing of God because it marks a moment when you are truly experiencing His presence. God wants to anoint you so that you can be a true instrument for His use in the Kingdom. You only need to stay focused and learn from Him. This is your time alone and it marks an opportunity to clearly hear the purpose of your journey and experience the great abundance found within the Scriptures.

> *He split the rocks in the wilderness, and gave them drink in abundance like the depths. He also brought streams out of the rock, and caused waters to run down like rivers* (Psalm 78:15-16).

> *You visit the earth and water it, You greatly enrich it; the river of God is full of water; You provide their grain. For so You have prepared it. You water its ridges abundantly, You settle its furrows; You make it soft with showers, You bless its growth. You crown the year with Your goodness, and your paths drip with abundance. They drop on the pastures of the wilderness, and the little hills rejoice on every side. The pastures are clothed with flocks; the valleys also are covered with grain; They shout for joy, they also sing* (Psalm 65:9-13).

> *He turns rivers into a wilderness and the watersprings into dry ground; A fruitful land into barreness, for the wickedness of those who dwell in it. He turns a wilderness into pools of water, and dry land into watersprings* (Psalm 107:33-35).

You may wonder why having the anointing is so important. It is significant because as you enter the Promised Land, you will face numerous challenges. Just like the Israelites, you are promised a land of "milk and honey," yet you will need to capture it from the enemy. With the anointing you can break their power. Although it would be nice to imagine the Promised Land as a restful place, you can be assured your entry will not be peaceful. This is why you must enter as an anointed warrior, leader, and servant of God. To better understand this, let's examine what I identify as the kingdom principles.

Kings of This World

You need to appreciate that the Kingdom of God is in your midst and you are seated with Christ as I speak. In every kingdom a ruler must exist and since you are seated with Him, He made you to be a king. However, Jesus is the King of kings and in His Kingdom, His cadre also functions as priests.

> ***And has made us kings and priests*** *to His God and Father, to Him be glory and dominion forever and ever. Amen* (Revelation 1:6).

In the Old Testament to be a priest, a person had to be born into a priestly family. It is the same for a king. A person has to be born into a kingly family to be a king. Since you are a born-again Christian, your royal lineage is assured.

This is why God's plan for you in the wilderness was of transformation so that you would be brought from slavery which represents life in the flesh into a place of honor within His royal priesthood.

Functions of a King

To better understand the role and functions of a king, let's examine their actions.

Ruling

Kings rule, they exercise authority over others, establish order, and are charged to be good stewards of what God gives them. This authority then obligates them to secure and protect the people. Great kings exercise their authority yet rule with righteousness and mercy. They are confident in their power and do not rule with an authoritarian spirit. God's purpose of making kings is to restore this kind of headship on earth. Yet unlike earthly kings who are confined by territorial boundaries, your domain is wherever you are.

Building

Kings also build their domain in order to secure it and bring additional assets. Expansion happens because they demand results, and in your role you should appropriately demand and expect great results as well. This is why Jesus gave us the Great Commission. God wants to expand His Kingdom here on earth and since you are His son or daughter, God commissioned you to expand and multiply His Kingdom. He wants you to make this your priority in life. As His anointed ruler God has given you a new identity to pursue this call. First, God has given you a new name in Him.

> *He who overcomes, I will make him a pillar in the temple of My God, and he shall go out no more. I will write on him the name of My God and the name of the city of My God, the New Jerusalem, which comes down out of heaven from My God.* ***And I will write on him My new name*** (Revelation 3:12).

Second, God made you to be at the top. You are the head and not the tail.

> *And* ***the Lord will make you the head and not the tail; you shall be above only, and not be beneath****, if you heed the commandments of the Lord your God, which I*

> *command you today, and are careful to observe them* (Deuteronomy 28:13).

Not only has He made you the head but He has given you every asset He has to accomplish His purpose. Every spiritual blessing is already given to you. You are blessed because everything that belongs to God is yours.

> *Blessed be the God and Father of our Lord Jesus Christ,* ***who has blessed us with every spiritual blessing in the heavenly places in Christ*** (Ephesians 1:3).

As a Christian you are blessed because you are born from above. You already have every blessing God has to offer. You have all the resources to give to people. God gave you the Holy Spirit so that you can activate these blessings in your life. This is why the Holy Spirit anointing releases these blessings. Does this excite you? Does this encourage you? Does this show you what type of person you are in Christ?

You were given the Holy Spirit as an assurance of your salvation. He is a guarantee or a proof of your salvation.

> *In Him you also trusted, after you heard the word of truth, the gospel of your salvation; in whom also, having believed,* ***you were sealed with the Holy Spirit of promise, who is the guarantee of our inheritance*** *until the redemption of the purchased possession, to the praise of His glory* (Ephesians 1:13-14).

However you cannot just limit the Holy Spirit only to this. You cannot limit it to just salvation because it says something about an inheritance. There is also an inheritance that is given to you when you receive Jesus as Lord and Savior. You have the right to receive an inheritance from the Lord because of His Holy Spirit. It is not only a future inheritance but also a present one. God gave each believer the Holy Spirit so that we can be rulers of this earth and reign with Him, having dominion over Heaven and earth. This is why the Bible states that you are seated with Him in heavenly places.

The Purpose of the Anointing

The reason for your godly anointing is so that you can rule and reign with Him on earth, exercising His Kingdom authority. You are anointed and God supplies everything you need because you have access to Him as a fellow king and joint heir with Jesus Christ. The enemy tries to deceive you by lying about your identity in Christ so you need to constantly think about your position in Christ.

You are important because you have kingship inside of you.

You may be accustomed to living with a slave mentality, yet God calls you to live and rule as a king. That is why you need to continuously rejoice for you are no longer a slave. You are positioned with Christ in the heavenly places, already seated with Him. You are important because you have kingship inside of you. This is a vital truth that you need to know about the anointing.

The anointing is something that is done in the supernatural that cannot be done in the natural. Without living in the anointing, you will not be able to see the power of God working in your life. Through the anointing God will restore things back into your life.

Receiving the Anointing

I already mentioned that God wants to anoint you, but how do you receive it? In order for that to happen, you need to be in a place where the anointing is always present. It is through the wilderness experience that you receive the anointing because that is where it is present. It is hard to comprehend that the anointing is in a totally barren place. The truth of the matter is that the anointing is present when one is always dependent on the Lord.

Receiving the anointing is not automatic. You need to pay a price. However many desire to receive the anointing only if it is free. The anointing is so precious that God does not give it to anyone until a person has stripped off their old life. He wants to make sure that the person is fully committed to Him and His Kingdom.

There is a reason why God wants to give you His anointing. When you receive the anointing, you will be able to defeat all the enemies in the Promised Land. God is giving you the anointing to break the enemy's gates.

> *Blessing I will bless you, and multiplying I will multiply your descendants as the stars of the heaven and as the*

> *sand which is on the seashore; and your descendants shall possess the gate of their enemies* (Genesis 22:17).

This was a promise that God gave to Abraham because of his obedience. If you walk in obedience like Abraham, you also will have the power to possess the gate of your enemies. If you do not break the enemy's gates, you cannot win any battles. The Promised Land is not a peaceful place but is filled with many enemies. With the anointing you will be able to drive them out of the land.

> *For My Angel will go before you and bring you in to the Amorites and the Hittites and the Perizzites and the Canaanites and the Hivites and the Jebusites; and I will cut them off. You shall not bow down to their gods, nor serve them, nor do according to their works;* ***but you shall utterly overthrow them and completely break down their sacred pillars*** (Exodus 23:23-24).

The enemies that you need to destroy are your sins. Sins in your life distract you from fulfilling what God wants you to do. God has given you the anointing to have dominion over this world. This also includes all of your sins.

> *It shall come to pass in that day, that his burden will be taken away from your shoulder, and his yoke from your neck, and* ***the yoke will be destroyed because of the anointing oil*** (Isaiah 10:27).

The reason why many people are still in bondage is because they have not yet destroyed the sins in their life. They allow the sins to remain in their life. Just like the Israelites did not destroy all the enemies when God told them to, some do not destroy sins in their lives. People do not destroy the sins in their lives because they are still living in the flesh.

You will face all kinds of obstacles and temptations in life. Without the anointing you will not be able to defeat anything that comes your way. Once you receive the anointing, you must then be able to hold onto it. The problem is that you have a hole in your vessel. The living water inside of you is starting to spill out. You have to stop the leak in your life.

> *Be astonished, O heavens, at this, and be horribly afraid; Be very desolate, says the Lord. For My people have committed two evils:* ***They have forsaken Me, the fountain of living waters, and hewn themselves cisterns, broken cisterns that can hold no water****"* (Jeremiah 2:12-13).

That is why in order for you to receive and hold onto the anointing, you need to crucify your flesh daily. All your fleshly life must be crucified on the cross.

> ***Therefore, do not let sin reign in your mortal body,*** *that you should obey it in its lusts* (Romans 6:12).

We must receive the power of God before we cross over the Jordan River, the symbol of death. Unless we're crucified with Christ, we cannot receive the anointing. However, when we crucify our flesh, God makes us into clean vessels capable of carrying the anointing to others.

When God wants to make us into clean vessels, He first deals with the inside of our heart. We have to show no mercy toward the sin in our heart. We should not try to compromise because it will only spoil and ruin our lives.

This is why some do not have the fullness of God and need the anointing to break through. Only through the anointing can this be accomplished.

Points to Ponder

1. What does it mean to you to be an anointed warrior, leader, and servant of God? Are you ready?

2. *"Blessed be the God and Father of our Lord Jesus Christ,* ***who has blessed us with every spiritual blessing in the heavenly places in Christ."*** Ponder your spiritual blessings and thank Him for them.

3. Have you made compromises that have spoiled your blessings from Him?

Conclusion

MY prayer is that you will embrace and welcome the wilderness experience. The wilderness experience is for your benefit because it will prepare you for the next level or stage in your life. It is a time where you will learn more of God and taste that the Lord is good. God is getting ready to take you into a better place in His Kingdom. You just need to look forward and not look back.

God wants you to know that you have potential in His Kingdom. In order for that to happen, you have to be kingdom-minded. As hard as it might be, you have to unlearn all the things you have learned that are contrary to His Word. If you want to step forward in life, you need to let go of all that is holding you back.

As you embark on your wilderness experience, always remember that God is making you into the person He called you to be. You just need to see things through His eyes. When you do, you will realize that you are destined for a great future. It is a great time to be alive in the world because you will witness many great moves of God in your lifetime. God wants you to be bold and to fully trust Him during these times. God will always lead you through His Spirit and you will find that you are destined to enter into the Promised Land.

Always remember that your wilderness experience is for a season. It will not last a lifetime. Throughout this experience your obedience to the Lord is very crucial. It is imperative that you realize the importance of this experience in your life. Instead of running away, run toward what will better empower you to live a life that is pleasing to the Lord. Run toward the wilderness. God is there to supply all your needs. Do not fear, but be bold as you go through your season in the wilderness.

Appendix

Three Dimensions of Christian Maturity

FLESH	SOUL	SPIRIT
Egypt	Wilderness	Canaan
First Heaven	Second Heaven	Third Heaven
Court	Holy Place	Holy of Holies
Flesh	Soul	Spirit
Red Sea	(Baptism) Jordan	River (Anointing)
Feast of Passover	Feast of Pentecost	Feast of Tabernacles
Flesh Conscious	Self Conscious	God Conscious
Tree of Knowledge	Trees to feed Soul	Tree of Life
30-Fold	60-Fold	100-Fold
Baptism of water	Baptism of Holy Spirit	Baptism of fire (Glory to God)
Sin (Bondage)	Miracles	Promised Land
Way	Truth	Life

FLESH	**SOUL**	**SPIRIT**
Son	Spirit	Father
First day	Second day	Third day
Faith	Hope	Love
Milk	Bread	Meat
Prophet	Priest	King
For all Israel	For the Priest	For the High Priest
Children	Youth	Adult
Thanksgiving	Praise	Worship
David's first anointing	Second anointing	Third anointing
Workers	Warriors	Worshipers
Justification	Sanctification	Glorification

About the Author

ISRAEL Kim came to America in the early 1980s to obtain a doctorate degree in International Business. However, God called him instead to be a minister of the Gospel of Jesus Christ. Since 1984 he has been involved in ministry with the Southern Baptist denomination and later moved to an affiliation with the Assembly of God ministries. He is ordained under the International Ministerial Association and Apostolic Resource Ministries.

His ministry is based upon the leading of the Holy Spirit to represent the Heavenly Father. He has been providing apostolic and prophetic oversight to many churches and ministers in many different nations. As he has traveled across the world, thousands and thousands of souls have been saved, healed, and delivered in his ministry. Miracles, signs, and wonders have been manifested as part of his ministry—dead people have even been raised. During a meeting in Moscow, 1,200 people were miraculously healed in one night.

Throughout 23 years of ministry experience, he has provided a well-balanced, biblical approach to the restoration of the office of the apostle in which he has functioned for the last 17 years. With his wife he is the co-founder and currently serves as president of Apostles Ministries and executive director of Apostles Ministries Empowerment Network.

He formerly served as a dean of St. Petersburg Christian College, and he currently serves as the chancellor of Wagner Leadership Institute in Japan and the International School of Apostles. He has also taught at several seminaries and Bible colleges in several countries. He is a member of the International Coalition of Apostles and a member of the Apostolic Council for Educational Accountability. He is also an honorary member of Who's Who.

He is the author of *The Image of God* and he and his wife, Rebekah, and daughter, Gloria, reside in Sterling, Virginia.

Contact Information

APOSTLES MINISTRIES EMPOWERMENT NETWORK

Phone: 703-430-5527

Fax: 703-436-4914

E-mail: apostle7@4amen.org

INTERNATIONAL SCHOOL OF APOSTLES

1-5-3F, Minamisaiwai-cho, Saiwai-ku,

Kawasaki-shi, Kanagawa, Japan 212-0061

Tel/Fax: 81-44-533-1240 (Japan)

E-mail: isoa@cronos.ocn.ne.jp

www.4amen.org